Whittet Books Ltd
1 St John's Lane
Stansted
Essex CM24 8JU
Email: mail@whittetbooks.com

First published 2010
Text © People's Trust for Endangered Species 2010
See page 89 for photograph and illustration copyright
details.

A catalogue record for this publication is available from the
British Library.

ISBN 978 1 873580 81 3

Designed by Lodge Graphics

people's trust for **endangered species** |

Britain's Mammals

a concise guide

Authors: David Wembridge & Clare Poland Bowen
Editor: Jill Nelson
Picture Editor: Zoe Roden

Whittet Books

Contents

Foreword

Mammals are among the most popular of all wild creatures. Otters, hedgehogs, dormice – everyone has a soft spot for them. Our British species range from tiny bats and shrews to large deer and seals. But most are small, nocturnal and hard to see. Nevertheless, they often leave tell-tale signs of their presence and, with practice, we can all learn to spot the clues that remind us just how many mammals we have in this country. Standing in a wood, there could be a hundred or more within fifty metres of you.

Some mammals have been introduced from abroad and some, like the house mouse and brown rat, are pests, but they should not be confused with their harmless and often endearing country cousins. Even the rabbit, a major agricultural menace, is vital food for many predators and its nibbling teeth help to maintain valuable habitats rich in orchids and butterflies. The inconspicuous field vole is the main food for barn owls, weasels, pine martens and many others, yet few people have ever seen one.

Some species, like the dormouse, water vole, red squirrel and hedgehog, have suffered serious losses and now need help to prevent them sliding into extinction. Often it is not clear why they have declined. Guessing is no good: successful conservation needs real understanding based on thorough research. We also need to monitor animal numbers to warn us when something goes wrong. The plight of the water vole and red squirrel is a reminder of this. Both are already extinct across large areas and it may be too late to save them. If a species begins to decline, we need to act quickly. Other species, like the harvest mouse and water shrew, may have declined without us even knowing. With help, our precious mammals can prosper, despite increasing demands on our countryside. With careful management and your support we can continue to enjoy the pleasure of sharing Britain with badgers, otters and many other attractive and fascinating mammals.

Pat Morris

Senior Lecturer in Zoology at Royal Holloway, University of London, for many years, Dr Pat Morris has devoted his life to the study of mammals. He has written extensively about them and is a frequent contributor to natural history broadcasts on radio and television.

Introduction

What is a mammal?

Ask two people to think of a mammal and they may come up with very different animals: a giant blue whale or a pygmy shrew; a subterranean mole or an aerial pipistrelle bat. Mammals have evolved to occupy very different habitats on our planet and there is an enormous variety of them. But there are some characteristics that all mammals have in common and that are not shared with most other animals. These shared features put them in the group: Mammalia.

Mammals have hair on all or a part of their body. Humans have very sparse hair on their bodies and whales have even less, but they do have some.

Mammals are internally heated: we generate our own warmth to keep our body temperature constant and above that of the surroundings. Birds do this as well.

Mammals give birth to live offspring. Five species however – the duck-billed platypus and the spiny anteaters – are exceptions, laying eggs instead.

Female mammals produce milk to suckle their young. Before they are able to fend for themselves, offspring are fed and protected by their mother, and the young of some species learn how to forage or hunt from her or from another adult.

Britain's mammals

Compared with most of our continental neighbours, the British Isles occupy a peculiar position: we sit on outcrop, an archipelago. The mammal species in Britain are only some of the 235 European species. Those species that were here when Britain became an island about 11,000 years ago as the sea level rose are considered native. Many have arrived since as stowaways on trading ships or have been introduced deliberately, while others have become extinct.

There are over 60 resident wild mammal species in the UK or around its coasts. The aim of this book is to provide a brief account of these and of some that are no longer here. They represent a diverse and sometimes surprising group.

About this book

Species are grouped into nine taxonomic groups called orders, which contain closely related species:

Insectivores (Order Eulipotyphla)

Bats (Order Chiroptera)

Rodents (Order Rodentia)

Carnivores (Order Carnivora)

Deer and wild boar (Order Artiodactyla)

Rabbits and hares (Order Lagomorpha)

Marsupials

Seals (Order Pinnipedia)

Whales and dolphins (Order Cetacea)

Altogether, 68 species are described here, including native and introduced species. Some species that are now extinct in Britain are described separately at the end of the book.

This is not a definitive list of British mammals however: certain species, including some subspecies, free-living domesticated species (such as feral goats and ferrets), and cetaceans that have been recorded only occasionally around our coasts, have been omitted.

Each species description in this book has been presented in the following way:

Common name and scientific name of the species - the scientific name is always written in italics and has two parts: the first (with a capital) is the genus name, such as *Mustela*. The second (without a capital) is the species name, such as *erminea*. Together, they are sufficient to identify each species uniquely – in this case, *Mustela erminea*, the stoat. Names are often descriptive – that of the grey seal, *Halichoerus grypus*, for example, is a mixture of Greek and Latin, meaning 'little sea pig with a hooked-nose'.

An introduction - describes the species' appearance and features, including details of behaviour and diet for some species.

Head-body length - the length in centimetres or metres of a typical adult from the tip of the snout to the base of the tail.

Tail or ear length - the length of the tail or ears, sometimes given in comparison to the measurement above.

Weight - the weight in grammes or kilogrammes of a typical adult.

Lifespan - the age that most individuals live to in the wild; sometimes the maximum recorded age either of a wild or a captive animal is given.

Reproduction - details such as the time of year that animals mate and give birth and the age that offspring are weaned.

Diet - the main prey or food items.

Habitat - the type of environment a species usually lives in.

Predators - species that feed on the animal.

Threats - factors that are or may be a problem for the long-term survival of the population.

Status & conservation - whether a species is native or not, how common or scarce it is, whether it is of conservation concern, and particular legislation that protects it.

Population size & distribution - an estimate of the current population size (often with a large degree of uncertainty) and how it is changing in the long-term. Figures are given either for the UK, GB (England, Scotland and Wales) or for individual countries, depending on whether data is available for particular regions and on the range of the species. Estimates for population sizes and trends are taken from *Mammals of the British Isles: Handbook, 4th Edition* by S. Harris and D. W. Yalden (2008), *UK Mammals: Species Status and Population Trends* edited by Jessamy Battersby (2005) and updates from the Tracking Mammals Partnership (available from www.trackingmammals.org).

A map shows the distribution of the population in the British Isles or around its coast. The shaded area indicates where the species is present.

A glossary at the end of the book explains many of the terms used and others that might be encountered in books about mammals.

The aim of this book is to act as a quick and up-to-date reference guide to Britain's mammals. But it provides only a glimpse – any one of the species could fill a book by itself.

You can help Britain's mammals

Understanding the extent and abundance of wild species is vital to working out which are a priority for conservation effort so that action is taken before they face irreversible decline.

People's Trust for Endangered Species monitors a wide range of mammals annually and individual species, such as hedgehogs and stag beetles, every few years. We are mapping vital habitats such as orchards and hedgerows and we manage the national database of hazel dormouse populations in over 200 woodlands across England and Wales.

Recently our annual Mammals on Roads survey highlighted a worrying fall in hedgehog numbers so we have embarked on a practical campaign to find out what's going on and do something about it.

Wildlife monitoring is a great way for anyone to get involved in conservation. Can you help? There are surveys to suit everyone depending on how much commitment you can give. But even taking part in our most basic surveys – telling us whether you have seen a particular species recently – really does help to amass important information that's put to good use. For current surveys please visit our website, which also has more information about mammals and useful links to other conservation organisations.

www.ptes.org

Shrews, moles and hedgehogs

Present-day insectivores, such as shrews, moles and hedgehogs, still have many of the features of the earliest mammals. They have relatively small brains, primitive teeth and abdominal testes, for example – traits characteristic of their ancestors, hundreds of millions of years ago. Many though also have highly evolved characteristics, such as the spines of hedgehogs (and tenrecs) and the digging forelimbs of moles. Small and mostly nocturnal, insectivores feed mainly on insects and other invertebrates, which are sought out with a long, sensitive snout and a keen sense of smell.

There are six insectivore species in Britain, the largest being the hedgehog and the smallest the pygmy shrew, which weighs about as much as a one-penny coin.

Moles, shrews and hedgehogs are largely solitary animals. Hedgehogs have overlapping home ranges and do not defend a territory, while shrews are more vociferous in excluding others from their home-patch.

Traditionally, the golden moles of southern Africa and the tenrecs of Madagascar and Africa have been grouped with moles, shrews and hedgehogs, in the order Insectivora. However, a more recent taxonomy separates the two groups into the order Eulipotyphla (moles, shrews and hedgehogs) and the order Afrosoricida (golden moles and tenrecs).

In the UK, all shrews are partially protected by law, under the Wildlife and Countryside Act 1981, making it illegal to deliberately kill or trap them without an appropriate licence.

Hedgehog *Erinaceus europaeus*

Hedgehogs are our only spiny mammal and are immediately recognisable. They have around 5,000 closely-packed, hollow, creamy-white spines, becoming brown at the base and pure white at the tip. Just behind the point is a dark, chocolate-brown band. On their underside, hedgehogs have coarse, grey-brown fur. By rolling up into a tight ball and erecting their spines, hedgehogs can protect themselves from most natural enemies.

They have a short inconspicuous tail, small ears and relatively long legs, normally hidden under a 'skirt' of long hairs. They are usually thought of as slow animals but they can move up to 40 metres a minute. They are mostly active at night or after heavy rainfall, and use their keen sense of smell to find food and alert them to danger. Between November and the end of March, when food is scarce, hedgehogs hibernate to conserve energy, remaining largely inactive.

Head-body length	Up to 30 cm
Tail length	2 cm
Weight	450-1500 g
Lifespan	About a half die in their first year. Average lifespan is about two years; a small percentage reach five years.

Reproduction: Up to seven blind, spineless offspring are usually born between May and August in a nest of leaves and grass. Pure white spines appear soon after birth and are replaced within a few weeks by darker spines that grow through. The young are weaned at about four weeks and become independent shortly afterwards.

Diet: Mainly beetles, caterpillars and earthworms but also birds' eggs, other invertebrates and carrion.

Habitat: Woodland edges, hedgerows in meadowland and rough pasture. They avoid wet areas or large pine forests.

Predators: Occasionally badgers and foxes.

Threats: Habitat loss due to agricultural change; and pesticides, which reduce the abundance of prey. Road deaths may be important locally.

Status & conservation: Hedgehogs are native and locally common. In 2007, hedgehogs were made a priority species in the UK Biodiversity Action Plan.

Population size & distribution: GB population 1,100,000. The population trend is unknown but there is evidence that the population is declining. Hedgehogs are found throughout the British Isles, including urban areas, but are absent from some of the Scottish Islands.

Did you know?

Occasionally, some hedgehogs produce large amounts of frothy saliva and spread it over their spines. The purpose of this 'self-anointment' is still a mystery.

Mole *Talpa europaea*

Molehills are a familiar sight in the UK but few people have ever seen the animal responsible. Moles spend almost all of their life underground and are well adapted to a digging lifestyle. They have strong, shovel-like forelimbs and short, velvety fur that can lie in either direction, allowing them to move easily forwards and backwards through tunnels. In shallow soil, the burrows are largely on one level, but elsewhere the elaborate tunnel system may be multi-tiered, running from just below the surface to about a metre down and covering several thousand square metres. The tunnel system acts as a pit-fall trap, collecting earthworms and insect larvae, which are caught by the patrolling resident before they can escape. When prey is plentiful, moles may be inconspicuous because the existing tunnels provide enough food, but it is clear that there is a seasonal effect, with more molehills appearing in spring and autumn than at other times.

Head-body length	12-17 cm
Tail length	2-4 cm
Weight	70-130 g
Lifespan	Two to three years; very few survive to five years.

Reproduction: Moles breed from late February to June. Litters of three or four pups are born in April or May and are weaned at four or five weeks of age. They disperse shortly afterwards and are able to breed the following spring.

Diet: Mainly soil invertebrates such as earthworms, insect larvae, myriapods (such a centipedes and millipedes) and slugs. They will also feed on carrion.

Habitat: Deciduous woodland, permanent pasture and arable fields, as well as gardens.

Predators: Tawny owls and stoats.

Threats: Moles are considered a pest on agricultural land and are controlled by trapping. Poisoning with strychnine was banned in the UK in 2007.

Status & conservation: Native, common and widespread. They are not listed by the International Union for Conservation of Nature.

Population size & distribution: UK population 31 million. The population trend is unclear. There is an indication that numbers have declined since 2000. Moles are widespread on mainland Britain and the islands of Skye, Mull, Anglesey, Wight, Alderney and Jersey. They are absent from Ireland.

Did you know?
The amount of oxygen in the tunnel system can be only a third of that at the surface and, to deal with this, moles have more blood and twice as much haemoglobin, the oxygen-carrying pigment in blood, than other mammals of their size.

Common shrew *Sorex araneus*

Common shrews are one of Britain's most abundant mammals but they are rarely seen, as much of their time is spent beneath the leaf litter or in long vegetation. They have distinctive narrow pointed snouts and brown (never black) fur on their back, with a paler, grey underside. The tails of adults tend to be bare and are often scarred. Shrews use a network of runways through the vegetation and dig burrows or use those of other small mammals. They are active during the day and night, although are most active during darkness. One to two hour bursts of activity are followed by periods of rest, usually in the nest but sometimes cat-napping elsewhere. A high-pitched twitter can sometimes be heard while they forage, using their snout and whiskers to probe and sniff the soil to find food. They can locate prey up to 12 cm beneath the surface of the soil. They are solitary and aggressively defend their territories.

Head-body length	6-8 cm
Tail length	About half the body length
Weight	5-15 g
Lifespan	15-18 months; 50 per cent die within two months.

Reproduction: Mating occurs between April and August. One or two litters of four to eight young are born from May onwards and females may have several litters in a season. The young sometimes caravan behind their mother during trips out of the nest and are weaned by 25 days.

Diet: Invertebrates such as earthworms, spiders, slugs, insect larvae and beetles, as well as small vertebrates and carrion.

Habitat: Woodland, thick grass and hedgerows, particularly road verges and other grassy banks. They make nests under logs, grass tussocks or in the burrows of other species.

Predators: Mostly owls and raptors, but also stoats, weasels and foxes. Domestic cats frequently kill shrews but do not eat them.

Threats: Habitat loss due to changes in farming practices, agricultural pesticides and pollution.

Status & conservation: Native, widespread and common. The trapping and killing of shrews requires a licence.

Population size & distribution: UK population 41,700,000. The population trend is unknown. They are found throughout Britain but are absent from Ireland, Shetland, Orkney, the Outer Hebrides, the Isle of Man, Scilly Isles and Channel Islands.

Did you know?

Their small size means that shrews lose heat quickly, and in order to stay warm they have a high metabolic rate. As a consequence, they must eat nearly their own body weight in food every day and small changes in the availability of prey can threaten their survival.

Pygmy shrew *Sorex minutus*

Pygmy shrews are one of Britain's smallest mammals – only pipistrelle bats weigh as little. They have grey-brown fur, paler than that of common shrews, and a long, slightly hairy tail. Pygmy shrews are active both day and night, but rest frequently. They use a network of runways through the ground vegetation and, unlike common shrews, do not dig for prey beneath the soil surface. They are poor burrowers and instead use the burrows and runways of other small mammals. Shrews have energetic metabolisms and pygmy shrews consume one and a quarter times their body weight each day. They are solitary and territorial animals and are aggressive towards other individuals, emitting a high-pitched squeak and sometimes swiping their tail from side to side if they encounter another pygmy shrew.

Head-body length	4-6.5 cm
Tail length	3-4.5 cm
Weight	3.5-7 g; up to 10 g in the breeding season
Lifespan	12-18 months in the wild; few live through a second winter.

Reproduction: Mating occurs from April to August and litters of up to nine pups (typically four to six) are born between May and October. The young are weaned after about three weeks and become sexually mature the following spring. Females can have two or three litters each year. The mortality of young pygmy shrews is very high.

Diet: Invertebrates such as beetles, spiders, woodlice and flies. Unlike common shrews, they do not eat earthworms.

Habitat: Usually grassland, deciduous woodland and hedgerows where there is sufficient cover. They also inhabit compost heaps and other wild areas in gardens.

Predators: Mostly tawny and barn owls, but also stoats, weasels, foxes and cats.

Threats: Loss of ancient grassland and meadows.

Status & conservation: Native and common. The trapping and killing of shrews requires a licence.

Population size & distribution: GB population 8,600,000. The population trend is unknown. Pygmy shrews are widely distributed throughout Britain and most offshore islands, but they are absent from Shetland, the Scilly Isles and the Channel Islands. They are the only species of shrew to be found in Ireland.

Did you know?

Like other shrews, pygmy shrews are unpalatable to many predators because of an unpleasant smelling secretion from their scent glands. Domestic cats frequently catch and kill shrews but will not eat them. There is no evidence that predators learn to avoid the musky scent, however, so it is unlikely to provide much protection for the shrew.

Water shrew *Neomys fodiens*

Water shrews are well adapted to an aquatic lifestyle: they have a dark brown (almost black), waterproof coat of short fur, and ears (visible as white tufts) that can close in the water. A fringe of stiff silvery hairs runs the length of the underside of the tail, which they use as a rudder, and their hind feet have similar fringes. They can dive to depths of over 70 cm, and hunt underwater as well as on land. Water shrews are mostly nocturnal and are particularly active just before dawn. They travel up to 160 metres along the water's edge to find food and shelter, and dig extensive networks of small burrows and chambers, about 2 cm wide, which they line with grass and leaves. They do not hibernate but are active through the winter.

Head-body length	6-10 cm
Tail length	5-8 cm
Weight	8-23 g
Lifespan	14-19 months; most adults die at the end of the breeding season.

Reproduction: Breeding extends through April to September, with a peak in May and June. One or two litters of 3-15 young are born each breeding season and some females may breed in their first calendar year. The young are weaned at about four weeks but stay with their mother for a further two weeks.

Diet: Mainly freshwater crustaceans such as shrimps, caddis-fly larvae and small snails, but also small fish, frogs and earthworms.

Habitat: Mainly the banks of fast-flowing, clear, unpolluted water, but also lakes, reed-beds, fens and marshes. They are often present in gardens.

Predators: Occasionally owls, kestrels, foxes, large fish and cats.

Threats: Habitat loss through water pollution.

Status & conservation: Native and locally common. The trapping and killing of shrews requires a licence.

Population size & distribution: GB population 1,900,000. The population trend is unknown but numbers are possibly declining. Water shrews are widely distributed in mainland Britain, particularly in central and southern England. They are scarce in the Scottish Highlands and absent from Ireland and the Isle of Man, and most of the small islands.

Did you know?

Like shrews in the genus *Sorex*, water shrews have teeth that are red-tipped but, unlike other species in Britain, they have venomous saliva that is capable of paralysing prey such as small fish and frogs.

Lesser white-toothed (or Scilly) shrew
Crocidura suaveolens

Lesser white-toothed shrews are only found on the Isles of Scilly, Jersey and Sark. As their name suggests, they have white teeth instead of the red-tipped ones of other shrews. They have light grey-brown fur, large ears and bristly hairs interspersed with long, white ones, covering their tail. They have adapted to life on the seashore, feeding on small crustaceans on the beach at low tide, as well as small invertebrates in the soil. Tunnels are made through the leaf litter and they are often active under logs and heaps of brushwood or stone. They emit a soft, continuous twittering while foraging or exploring, but produce a sharp squeak if threatened or alarmed. Lesser white-toothed shrews are more social than other shrew species and several adults will often share the same nest.

It is likely that lesser white-toothed shrews were introduced to Britain by Iron Age traders from France or northern Spain.

Head-body length	5-8 cm
Tail length	2.5-5.5 cm
Weight	3.5-7 g; up to 10 g in the breeding season
Lifespan	12-18 months in the wild; few live through a second winter.

Reproduction: Mating occurs from March to September and two to four litters of up to five pups (fewer than litters of other shrew species) are born after a gestation of 24-32 days. Some offspring breed later in the same calendar year, but most do not reach sexual maturity until the following spring.

Diet: Soil invertebrates such as earthworms and beetles, and small crustaceans such as sandhoppers.

Habitat: Tall vegetation including bracken and in hedgebanks, as well as sand dunes, scrub and boulders of coastal areas. They nest under logs, between boulders or in abandoned mouse burrows.

Predators: Barn owls, kestrels, domestic cats, stoats and weasels.

Threats: No significant threats.

Status & conservation: Non-native and localised. The trapping and killing of shrews requires a licence.

Population size & distribution: 40,000-99,000. The population trend is unknown. They occur on the islands of Scilly, Jersey and Sark (Channel Islands), Sein, Ouessant and Yeu.

Did you know?

During their first few outings from the nest, young Scilly shrews will use their mouth to grip the tail of the sibling in front, forming a caravan procession behind their mother. This helps the mother to keep her large charge together while searching for food.

Rodents

Worldwide, there are more than 2,100 species of rodent – about 41 per cent of all mammal species. In Britain, they account for about a quarter of mammal species and are among the rarest and the most abundant. Some, like grey squirrels, are considered, by a minority perhaps, to be a pest. Others, like red squirrels, are among conservationists' greatest concerns.

The Latin word *rodere* means 'to gnaw' and gnawing is something that distinguishes rodents from other groups of mammals. They have distinctive front teeth, called incisors, which grow continuously so that the teeth are replaced as they are worn away.

There are 15 species of rodent in Britain, eight of which are native. The others, either stowaways with traders or brought over intentionally, have since become naturalised. Orkney voles (a subspecies of common voles) and house mice reached Britain by the early Bronze, and Iron Age respectively, while edible dormice and grey squirrels are comparative newcomers.

The variety of different rodent species is a measure of their evolutionary success. Most are seed-eaters while some, such as voles, are herbivores. Many have varied diets, such as hazel dormice which take advantage of buds, insects and seeds as they come into season. In turn, rodents are the major food source for many other animals, the prey of predators such as owls, stoats, and weasels.

Hazel dormice and red squirrels are fully protected by the Wildlife and Countryside Act 1981. It is therefore illegal to trap or kill them without an appropriate licence.

Red squirrel *Sciurus vulgaris*

Red squirrels have a red-brown coat (sometimes appearing quite grey) and, in winter, characteristic long, red tufts of fur on top of their ears. They spend almost all of their time in the tree canopy and rarely come down to the ground. High up in the branches, they build spherical nests (called dreys) from twigs, lined with moss, dried leaves or grass. They are solitary animals that are active during the day, particularly at dawn and dusk. Red squirrels can store little fat and need to eat regularly; they spend up to four-fifths of the time that they are active, feeding and foraging. They have dextrous front feet, which they use to manipulate their food. Squirrels are active throughout the winter and during late summer and autumn will cache tree seeds and conifer cones just below the soil surface to eat when food is scarce. Seeds and nuts carried in the mouth are marked with a scent by cheek glands, helping the squirrel locate the hoard at a later date.

Head-body length	18-24 cm
Tail length	14-20 cm
Weight	250-300 g
Lifespan	Up to seven years

Reproduction: Litters of one to six kits are born from February to April and a second litter from May to July. The young are weaned by 10 weeks and may stay with mothers over winter.

Diet: Pine cones, seeds, fruit, tree shoots, buds, flowers, berries, bark and lichens.

Habitat: Generally large pine forests, usually over 50 hectares in size, but also other types of woodland.

Predators: Polecats, pine martens, wildcats, some owls and goshawks.

Threats: Competition with grey squirrels; loss of woodland habitat; and disease (squirrel poxvirus).

Status & conservation: Native but many current populations have a recent Scandinavian ancestry from introductions in the 1960s. They are classified as Near Threatened in England, Wales and Northern Ireland but are locally common in Scotland. They are a priority species in the UK Biodiversity Action Plan.

Population size & distribution: GB population 161,000 (Scotland, 121,000). The red squirrel population has declined steadily since the introduction of grey squirrels, in both its range and size. In southern England, isolated populations remain on Brownsea and Furzey islands (Dorset) and the Isle of Wight; and populations are present in Wales, Lancashire, North Yorkshire, Durham, Cumbria and Norfolk. They are abundant in large parts of Scotland but absent from most of the Scottish islands. Red squirrels were relatively common until the 1940s.

Did you know?
Red squirrels will harvest fungi and dry the fruiting bodies in trees, to be eaten later.

Grey squirrel *Sciurus carolinensis*

Grey squirrels were introduced from North America in the 19th and 20th centuries. They are bolder and larger than red squirrels and, as their name suggests, have predominantly grey fur, although they can sometimes have patches of red. They are active during the day and are extremely agile climbers, although will spend a lot of time on the ground foraging. They sometimes bury excess food, often at the base of trees, to feed on during the cold winter months. They can be considered a pest because of damage to trees caused by stripping the bark, and because in gardens they may raid bird tables and feed on fruit crops or bulbs.

Head-body length	24-28 cm
Tail length	19-24 cm
Weight	400-600 g
Lifespan	Up to nine years

Reproduction: Two litters of two to four kits are born each year, one from February to April and the other from July to November. The young are weaned between 8 to 10 weeks.

Diet: Acorns, beech mast, flowers, nuts, bulbs, tree bark and tree shoots.

Habitat: Primarily woodland, but now common in urban areas, including gardens and parks.

Predators: Few natural predators.

Threats: Road traffic accidents.

Status & conservation: Non-native and common.

Population size & distribution: GB population 2,600,000 (England, 2,000,000). The population is likely to be increasing. Grey squirrels are widely distributed throughout England and Wales and are edging their way into Scotland and Northern Ireland. They are absent from Europe except for a small but expanding area in Northern Italy.

Did you know?
Grey squirrels are capable of running easily up and down trees by virtue of their strong claws and 'double jointed' ankles, which allow their feet to face forwards or backwards.

Bank vole *Myodes glareolus* (formerly *Clethrionomys glareolus*)

The smallest of the UK's voles, bank voles have a reddish-chestnut coat with a dirty white underside. Their tail is under half the length of their body and they have a blunt nose with small eyes and ears. At first sight, they can be confused with field voles, which are greyer, or wood mice, which have a longer tail and bound rather than scurry. Bank voles are active during both the day and night, and forage over distances of up to 50 metres. Males sometimes travel further to find a mate. They make their nests in shallow burrows that they dig just beneath the ground and which they line with leaves, grasses, moss or feathers. They are very nimble climbers and often climb up bushes to nibble fruit and buds.

Head-body length	8-12 cm
Tail length	Less than half the body length
Weight	14-40 g
Lifespan	Up to 18 months

Reproduction: Litters of three to five blind, hairless young are born between April and October and become independent within nine weeks. Over half of those born early in the season will die before they are four months old.

Diet: Grass, roots, fruit such as apples, seeds, and also insects and earthworms.

Habitat: Broadleaf woodland, scrubland, hedgerows and sometimes gardens where there is plenty of ground cover and food.

Predators: Tawny owls, weasels and foxes.

Threats: Habitat loss and agricultural pesticide use.

Status & conservation: Native to Great Britain; populations in Ireland were accidentally introduced in the 1950s. Common and widespread. Bank voles are not legally protected in the UK and have no conservation designation.

Population size & distribution: UK population 75 million. The population trend is unknown. Bank voles are widely distributed throughout Britain and the south west of Ireland.

Did you know?

A close relative (subspecies) of the bank vole is present on Skomer Island off the south west coast of Wales. The Skomer vole arrived there hundreds of years ago and is twice the size of its mainland relative.

Field (or Short-tailed) vole *Microtus agrestis*

Field voles are an important small mammal in Britain because so many predators depend on them as a food source. They look very similar to the bank vole but have longer dark brown fur, smaller ears and shorter tails. Field voles are active both day and night, but especially at dusk and dawn. They can be aggressive and often fight with each other, emitting loud squeaks to defend their territory. They are poor climbers, using instead a network of small runways which lead to underground tunnel entrances. They have very acute senses of smell and hearing, which they use to find food and evade predators.

Head-body length	8-13 cm
Tail length	A third of the body length
Weight	14-50 g
Lifespan	Up to two years

Reproduction: Litters of four to six young are born between April and September, and each female may have up to seven litters a year. The young are weaned by three weeks, when the female abandons the nest and finds a new territory where she will breed again.

Diet: Mainly grasses and herbaceous plants, but also bark in winter and occasionally insect larvae.

Habitat: Mainly grassy fields, but also mountain heath, open woodland, dunes and young forestry plantations. Females build a spherical nest of finely shredded grass at the base of a tussock or under logs.

Predators: Barn owls, pine martens, foxes, stoats, weasels, kestrels and snakes.

Threats: Loss of rough grassland habitat; and increased grazing from rabbits.

Status & conservation: Native and locally common.

Population size & distribution: GB population 75 million. The population trend is unknown but numbers have probably declined in the last century. Field voles are widely but patchily distributed throughout England, Scotland and Wales, but are absent from Ireland, the Isle of Man, Channel Islands, Scilly Isles and many Scottish islands.

Did you know?
Field voles mark their runways with a strong scent to warn away other voles. The markings though are visible in the ultra-violet part of the spectrum, alerting birds overhead to their presence.

Water vole *Arvicola amphibious* (formerly *Arvicola terrestris*)

Water voles are the largest species of vole in Britain and are sometimes mistaken for brown rats, which can be found in a similar habitat. Water voles have glossy brown or black fur and a blunt muzzle with small, black eyes. Their ears are rounded and almost hidden, and they have a dark, slightly furry tail. They are mostly active during the day, sitting on their hind feet and feeding on grass stalks held in their front paws. If they are disturbed, they dive into the water with a characteristic 'plop' sound. When they swim, their head and back are visible.

Water voles have undergone one of the most serious declines of any wild mammal in Britain during the 20th century. The intensification of agriculture in the 1940s and 1950s caused the loss and degradation of habitat but the most rapid period of decline was during the 1980s and 1990s as American mink spread. Between 1990 and 1998, the population fell by almost 90 per cent.

Head-body length	12-20 cm
Tail length	About half the length of the body
Weight	Up to 300 g
Lifespan	Few survive two winters.

Reproduction: Litters of two to eight blind, hairless pups are born from April to September and females can have up to five litters in a year. The young are weaned at about three weeks.

Diet: Grasses, common reeds, sedges, less frequently rushes in spring and summer; roots, tree bark and fruit in autumn and winter. Very occasionally insects and other invertebrates are eaten.

Habitat: Grassy banks along slow moving rivers, lakes, ponds and marshland. They dig burrows in steep grassy banks, which often include underwater entrances.

Predators: Mink, foxes, otters, stoats, weasels, owls, herons, pike and cats. Golden eagles in the Scottish Highlands.

Threats: Habitat loss from unsympathetic riverside management; water pollution; and predation by the American mink in the last 30 years.

Status & conservation: Native and locally common but vulnerable to extinction in the UK. They are a priority species in the UK Biodiversity Action Plan. Since 1998, Schedule 5 of the Wildlife and Countryside Act 1981 makes it an offence to intentionally damage or obstruct access to water vole burrows, but the Act does not protect the animals themselves. A reintroduction programme is currently underway.

Population size & distribution: GB population 875,000. A long-term decline has continued in the last 10 years. Water voles are found throughout England, Wales and Scotland but are absent from Ireland and most offshore islands except Anglesey and the Isle of Wight.

Did you know?
Genetic studies have shown Scottish water voles to be more akin to Iberian populations, while English and Welsh water voles are more closely related to populations in East Europe.

Orkney vole *Microtus arvalis orcadensis*

Orkney voles are a subspecies of common voles, and have developed over thousands of years on the Orkney Islands in Scotland. They look very similar to field voles but are larger and have shorter, paler brown fur. Their ears are almost bald inside but furry at the top. Orkney voles are active both day and night, but especially at dusk and dawn. They run quickly and often stand up on their hind legs to scan their surroundings. They burrow shallow tunnel systems and small chambers in which to nest and store food. They return to their nests every few hours to rest. They are good swimmers. Orkney voles are an important food source for the birds of prey on the islands.

Head-body length	9-12 cm
Tail length	Nearly a third of the body length
Weight	Up to 100 g
Lifespan	Up to 18 months

Reproduction: Two to four litters of 2-12 pups are born between March and September and the young are weaned by about three weeks. Both males and females spend much time in the nest with the young, grooming them and retrieving them if they are dislodged.

Diet: Mainly grasses and herbaceous plants.

Habitat: Mainly grassy banks along roads and ditches and grazed pastures but also found on moorland and in bogs. They are not as reliant on long grass for cover as common voles, as they often burrow. They also use stones of old ruined buildings as shelter.

Predators: Hen harriers, stoats, kestrels and short-eared owls.

Threats: Habitat loss and fragmentation due to agricultural pressure.

Status & conservation: Non-native and common where they occur.

Population size & distribution: Scotland, 1 million. The population is thought to be stable. Orkney voles are present on eight of the Orkney islands.

Did you know?

A slightly different island subspecies of common vole (with pure grey fur on its underside) is present on Guernsey in the Channel Islands.

Wood (or Long-tailed field) mouse
Apodemus sylvaticus

Wood mice are one of the most abundant and ubiquitous wild rodents in Britain. They have yellowish-brown fur on their backs and pale grey fur on their underside. They have a small yellowish patch of fur between their front legs, but less pronounced than in yellow-necked mice. They have large eyes and ears, and a long, dark, hairless tail, which they trail on the ground behind them. Wood mice are mostly nocturnal, run fast and are very agile climbers. They dig underground burrows in which to nest that probably survive from one generation to the next. Food is stored in chambers for the winter months.

Head-body length	8-11 cm
Tail length	As long as the head and body
Weight	16-18 g in winter; 25-27 g in summer
Lifespan	Up to 20 months

Reproduction: Litters of four to eight young are born between March and November, and females can have up to six litters in a year. The young are weaned by three weeks and are sexually mature within two months.

Diet: Mainly seeds, but also buds, fruits, nuts, snails, insects, fungi, moss and tree bark.

Habitat: Primarily a woodland species, but they are found in most habitats, including arable land, ungrazed grassland, hedgerows and field margins, as well as gardens and buildings.

Predators: Owls, foxes, mustelids, kestrels and cats.

Threats: Agricultural pesticides.

Status & conservation: Native, widespread and common.

Population size & distribution: GB population 38 million. The population trend is unknown. The wood mouse is widely distributed throughout Great Britain and Ireland, including most of the large islands and many of the small ones.

Did you know?
Wood mice spend a lot of time grooming. They wipe their face and ears with their forefeet and pass their tails through their mouths. Males and females will often groom each other.

Yellow-necked mouse *Apodemus flavicollis*

Yellow-necked mice can be easily confused with the more common wood mice, and the two were only identified as separate species in 1834. Yellow-necked mice are larger and their dorsal fur is more orange in colour than that of wood mice. The yellow band of fur between their front legs joins the brown fur on either side, which it doesn't do in wood mice. They are nocturnal and are good climbers, travelling large distances in trees in search of buds, seeds or small insects. They often jump around energetically and are more likely to bite if they are handled. They make use of extensive burrow systems, mostly within 50 cm of the surface but sometimes over a metre deep, in which food is stored. Yellow-necked mice are more tolerant of each other than wood mice, and three or four adults may nest together in winter.

Head-body length	10-12 cm
Tail length	Longer than body
Weight	25-45 g
Lifespan	Few survive longer than 12 months

Reproduction: Up to three litters of 4-11 pups are born each year between February and October. The young are weaned by four weeks. Those born in the spring are sexually mature at about 10 weeks and can breed in the same calendar year; autumn-born offspring usually reproduce only in the following spring.

Diet: Insects, seedlings, buds, fruit and insect larvae.

Habitat: Mainly woodlands, but also hedgerows and orchards. They are sometimes found inside buildings, such as food stores and garden sheds, particularly in winter.

Predators: Barn and tawny owls, stoats, weasels, badgers, foxes and cats.

Threats: Loss of ancient woodland habitat.

Status & conservation: Native and locally common.

Population size & distribution: GB population 750,000. The population trend is unknown. Yellow-necked mice are common only in the south and southeast of England, and central Wales. Records from Neolithic and Roman sites suggest that they were once more widespread than they are now. They are absent from Scotland and Wales.

Did you know?

Yellow-necked mice sometimes escape predators by jumping almost a metre in height, over eight times their own body length.

Harvest mouse *Micromys minutus*

Harvest mice are the smallest rodents in Europe and the only British mammal to have a prehensile tail, able to grasp plant stems as they move through long vegetation. They have a reddish-yellow coat with a distinct white underside, small hairy ears and a much blunter nose than other mice. They are mostly nocturnal, although are active during the day in warm summer months. They build several grass nests throughout a season for breeding, sleeping and resting. Harvest mice are less active in winter but do not hibernate; they stay close to the ground for warmth and insulation, and store food to sustain them through the winter months.

Head-body length	5-8 cm
Tail length	As long as the head and body
Weight	5-11g
Lifespan	Up to 18 months

Reproduction: Harvest mice breed between May and October, producing several litters in a year. Litters of three to eight pups are born after a gestation of 17-19 days. The young are weaned by about two weeks.

Diet: Grass seeds, fruit, berries, grain and sometimes insects in the winter.

Habitat: Cornfields, hedgerows, reed-beds, brambles, long grass and sometimes open fields.

Predators: Barn owls, stoats, weasels and crows.

Threats: Severe winters and starvation; farming practices such as combine harvesting and stubble burning; and pesticides.

Status & conservation: Probably an introduction after the last glaciation. They can be quite common locally.

Population size & distribution: UK population 1,425,000. The population trend is unknown but it is thought that numbers have declined in the last 40 years and they are now rare. They mainly occur in southern and eastern England, with a few records in the Midlands, the north of England and southern Scotland. They are absent from Ireland.

Did you know?

Harvest mice shred grasses by pulling them through their teeth and use the strips to weave a hollow nest, about the size of a tennis ball, about 50-100 cm above the ground and secured to grass stems.

House mouse *Mus domesticus*

House mice have long been associated with humans and they have spread along trade routes across much of the world: apart from our own species, house mice are thought to be the most widespread mammals in the world. They have been present in Britain since at least the Iron Age. They have grey-brown fur, large pink ears and a long, hairless tail. They can be distinguished from wood and yellow-necked mice by their narrower head and smaller eyes. House mice are mainly nocturnal, usually sleeping during daylight hours. Where food and shelter are scarce, house mice may range over areas of 200 square metres or more; when resources are readily available, home ranges may be as small as five square metres. They are territorial and when individuals are crowded, only a few dominant males hold territories and breed, frequently fighting with each other.

Head-body length	6-10 cm
Tail length	As long as the head and body
Weight	12-22 g
Lifespan	Up to 18 months in the wild but few survive longer than six months.

Reproduction: Five to ten litters of four to eight pups are born in a year. The young are weaned by two weeks and become sexually mature by five to six weeks. In her lifetime, a female may produce about 40 offspring.

Diet: Mainly grain and fruit, but also insects and other invertebrates.

Habitat: Competition with other small mammals means that house mice are rarely found in woodland in Britain; their best known habitat is the built environment, such as houses, food stores, farm buildings and rubbish tips. They also occur in arable land.

Predators: Barn owls, stoats, weasels, rats and domestic cats.

Threats: Severe cold; they are killed as a pest.

Status & conservation: Non-native and locally abundant.

Population size & distribution: GB population 5,400,000. The population has been stable over the last 25 years. House mice are widely distributed throughout Britain and Ireland, including most inhabited small islands.

Did you know?
House mice can be seen in the tunnels of the London Underground system. They thrive in the warmth and on the rubbish thrown away by commuters.

23

Hazel (or Common) dormouse
Muscardinus avellanarius

Hazel dormice have golden-brown fur and large black eyes and, distinctively, they are the only small British mammal with a furry tail. They are nocturnal and spend almost all of their time in the branches of trees during the summer, rarely coming down to the ground. They have sometimes been found asleep in old bird nests but they weave their own nests (often in brambles or other shrubs) from strips of honeysuckle bark or a similar plant, surrounded by a layer of green leaves. When conditions are cold or wet, or if food is scarce, dormice curl up into a ball and go into a state similar to hibernation for a short time (called torpor) in order to save energy. Between October and May dormice hibernate in nests beneath the leaf litter on the forest floor or in the base of hedgerows.

Head-body length	6-9 cm
Tail length	A little shorter than the body
Weight	15-35 g
Lifespan	Up to five years

Reproduction: Litters of three to seven pups are typically born in July or August but may be as early as May or as late as October. Juveniles leave their mother's nest after about two months and must be at least 15 g in weight to survive hibernation. Dormice usually have a single litter each year but if the summer is long, may produce a second.

Diet: Flowers, honeysuckle and pollen in spring; fruits, hazelnuts, beechmast and sweet chestnuts in the autumn. They will also eat small insects such as aphids.

Habitat: Deciduous woodland with new growth, scrub, and large, overgrown hedgerows. They are sometimes found in conifer plantations.

Predators: Occasionally owls, weasels and cats but they have few natural predators.

Threats: Habitat loss and fragmentation; climate change.

Status & conservation: Native and localised. Hazel dormice are rare and vulnerable to extinction in the UK. They are a priority species in the UK Biodiversity Action Plan and are protected under the Wildlife and Countryside Act 1981.

Population size & distribution: UK population 45,000. There has been a long-term decline in numbers, which continues. There is an indication however that the decline in recent years is less steep. Hazel dormice are patchily distributed, mostly in southern counties of England and in Wales.

Did you know?

Wood mice, bank voles and hazel dormice feed on hazelnuts by gnawing a round hole in the shell and each leaves distinctive marks. The tooth-marks of dormice run parallel to the edge of the hole, rather than outwards from its centre, so that the rim looks smooth, and there are few tooth-marks elsewhere on the nut. In contrast, the tooth-marks of mice and voles run outwards, so that the rim of the hole looks like the milled edge of a coin.

Fat (or Edible) dormouse *Glis glis*

Fat dormice are native to Central Europe and were introduced into a park in Hertfordshire by Walter Rothschild in 1902. They look like small, fat grey squirrels with long, black whiskers and large eyes and ears. They are much larger than native, hazel dormice and are called 'edible' because they were often eaten, especially in Roman times. Edible dormice are nocturnal and spend most of their time in the tree canopy or buildings. During the day, they rest in nests, similar to squirrel dreys, in trees or roof spaces. They are often found in groups and can sometimes become a nuisance. Up to 30 have been removed from the attic of a single house. They come down to the ground to hibernate in response to low temperatures and reduced food availability, finding sites under tree roots or in the burrows of other animals. They hibernate from September until May.

Head-body length	13-19 cm
Tail length	12-15 cm
Weight	50-250 g
Lifespan	Up to eight years in the wild

Reproduction: A single litter of up to usually seven blind and hairless pups is born between mid-July and September. Their fur is well developed by 16 days and they open their eyes about a week later. They stay in the nest for about 30 days. Mothers and daughters may share a nest and nurse their young communally.

Diet: Flower buds, insects, tree bark, beech mast, fruits (especially blackberries and elderberries), acorns and occasionally birds' eggs.

Habitat: Extensive and well-connected sites of mixed woodland including beech and conifer trees; they frequently live in buildings, including occupied houses.

Predators: Tawny owls, stoats, weasels and cats.

Threats: Poor mast years cause high mortality in juveniles during the winter.

Status & conservation: Non-native and locally common. They are classified as Least Concern on the IUCN Red List.

Population size & distribution: England population 10,000. The population trend is unknown. Fat dormice are common in the Chilterns in England, largely within 35 km of Tring Park where they were introduced at the beginning of the 20th century.

Did you know?

If a predator grabs a fat dormouse by the tail, the skin of the tail comes off allowing the dormouse to escape. The dormouse can only do this once, however, because the exposed tailbones soon break-off and do not re-grow.

Brown (or Common) rat *Rattus norvegicus*

Brown rats are thought to have been introduced into Britain in the 18th century, accidental stowaways in shipping from Russia. They are intelligent and highly adaptable animals, and have lodged alongside humans for millennia. Brown rats have grey-brown fur and a long, scaly tail, which is used to help them balance. They live in large colonies made up of smaller social units or 'clans'. High ranking males occupy the best positions, close to food sources. Brown rats tend to use the same routes to get from one place to another and in buildings the runs are apparent as dark smears. They are excellent swimmers and divers, and agile climbers, occasionally climbing trees. They dig extensive burrows that may be used for generations.

Head-body length	Up to 28 cm
Tail length	A little shorter than head-body length
Weight	200-400 g
Lifespan	Up to 18 months

Reproduction: Litters of 6-11 pups are born and are weaned by three weeks. Young rats are grey and can be confused with mice. They breed throughout the year and females can have up to five litters in a year.

Diet: Cereals and root crops in agricultural land; meat, fish, bones, fruit and invertebrates in urban areas.

Habitat: Brown rats are typically associated with farms, rubbish tips, sewers, urban waterways and warehouses but they also live in hedgerows and cereal crops. They dig burrows in banks, leaving heaps of earth nearby.

Predators: Cats, foxes and owls predate young rats but adults have few natural predators.

Threats: Road traffic accidents; they are killed as a pest.

Status & distribution: Native and common.

Population size & distribution: GB population 6,790,000. The population trend is unknown. Brown rats are widely distributed throughout the UK but are absent from most exposed mountain regions.

Did you know?
Rats spend a lot of their time washing and grooming: although they often live in rubbish tips and sewers (habitats created by humans), they are fastidiously clean.

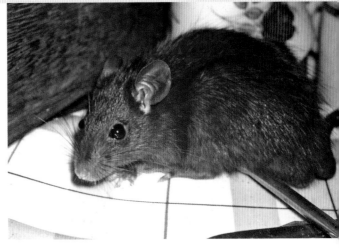

Black (or Ship) rat *Rattus rattus*

Black rats are one of the rarest mammals in Britain now, their numbers having diminished over the last fifty years as dockyards, which served as their last outpost, have been modernised. They reached Britain on trade ships in Roman times, having spread originally from India. Despite their name, their coats vary in colour from black to grey-brown. Ship rats are smaller than brown rats and have comparatively larger eyes and ears. They have longer, thinner tails and their ears are almost hairless, compared with the furry ears of brown rats. In towns, ship rats live only within buildings, such as dockside warehouses while, on islands, they occupy rocks and cliffs. They are mostly nocturnal and live in groups with a dominant male. Skilled and agile climbers, they can run along telephone wires, and prefer to make their nests high up in roof spaces, giving them their other name of roof rats. In the tropics, and reportedly on the Channel Islands, they also live in trees.

Head-body length	10-24 cm
Tail length	A little longer than head-body length
Weight	150-200 g
Lifespan	Up to 18 months

Reproduction: Up to five litters of on average five to eight pups are born between March and November.

Diet: Seeds, fruit and grain.

Habitat: Often inside large storage buildings, but also in grassy fields.

Predators: Domestic cats in urban areas, and elsewhere, most mammalian and avian predators.

Threats: Black rats have been gradually displaced by the larger brown rat, which is better adapted to withstand the cold in temperate countries. Rat-proof food stores have also hastened their disappearance.

Status & conservation: Non-native and very rare.

Population size & distribution: GB population 1,300 (up to 1,000 on the Shiant Islands, Hebrides). There may still be transient populations in Southwark in London, and Avonmouth, and some small populations on offshore islands. It is not known whether they are still present on the Channel Islands of Alderney and Sark.

Did you know?

Black rats were an unwitting carrier of plague (or Black Death), which killed around 40 per cent of people in Europe in the 14th century. The disease is caused by a bacterium and was spread most commonly by the bite of the fleas that lived on black rats.

European beaver *Castor fiber*

European beavers were once widespread in Great Britain and Europe but were hunted across their range for their fur and for their musk scented secretions, called castoreum. They were extinct in Britain by the 16th century and the European population was just 1,200 individuals in 1900. Since then, the population has partially recovered and there have been successful reintroductions to parts of France, southern Germany and Austria. In May 2009, three beaver families were released at separate sites in the Knapdale Forest in Argyll in Scotland as part of a trial, and have since begun breeding.

Beavers are excellent swimmers and dive for periods of five to six minutes, using their broad, flattened tail as a rudder. They burrow into the bank or use existing holes for dens (called lodges), which have entrances below the water level. If there are no suitable banks, lodges are built from branches, soil and woody debris. In addition, beavers construct dams, creating floodplains that extend the protection around their lodge and provide increased opportunities to forage.

Head-body length	75-90 cm
Tail length	28-38 cm
Weight	Up to 38 kg
Lifespan	Seven to eight years

Reproduction: Beavers breed mainly from December to April. Litters of usually two or three kits are born in May or June. The young learn to swim within hours and leave the nest at one to two months. They are weaned in their first summer but may not disperse until two years old. They are unlikely to breed successfully until their third year.

Diet: Aquatic and herbaceous plants in summer and bark of broad-leaved trees in winter. They sometimes fell young trees in October and November to store as food during the winter.

Habitat: Areas with year-round access to water – ideally, slow-flowing rivers or lakes with deciduous woodland on their banks. They can colonise non-ideal habitat by dam-building, which extends foraging habitat.

Predators: Historically, wolf and lynx; fox and some raptors such white-tailed eagle.

Threats: They were extensively hunted in the past.

Conservation & status: Once native, extinct for over 400 years in Scotland and longer in England and Wales. The existing small population is made up of individuals introduced from Norway.

Population size & distribution: At least two breeding pairs and two kits from the 11 adults introduced. Beavers were once widely distributed in Great Britain but were never present in Ireland.

Did you know?
Beavers are not very vocal, sometimes growling or hissing, but they warn each other of danger by slapping their flattened tails on the surface of the water as they dive to escape.

Rabbits and hares

Lagomorphs are herbivores with large, chisel-like front teeth that grow and are worn away continuously. There are three species of lagomorphs in the UK: rabbits, brown hares and mountain hares.

Until 1912, rabbits and hares were put in the same taxonomic group as that of mice and voles. More recent studies of their genes have shown that they are more closely related to primates and tree shrews than they are to the rodent family.

From a distance, hares and rabbits look similar but in several respects they are very different. Hares are bigger and have longer legs and ears than rabbits. They spend their lives above ground, unlike rabbits, which dig a network of burrows. Newborn hares, called leverets, are more precocious than newborn rabbits; without the protection of a burrow, they need to be mobile quickly. They are born with fur and are able to see and move about within hours of birth.

Rabbits and hares are very alert animals that have long mobile ears, with which they listen for predators. Escape is their main form of defence as their long back legs are adapted for running at speed.

The total weight of all UK rabbits is more than the collective weight of any other terrestrial wild mammal in the UK (perhaps twice as much as red deer) and they have a far-reaching impact on the natural landscape. Their grazing can be a problem for forestry and agriculture but elsewhere it maintains a particular community of species. They stop woody seedlings becoming established and prevent large areas of chalk downland becoming scrub. The short sward provides a habitat for birds such as woodlarks and lapwings, and breeding sites for sand lizards. After myxomatosis in the 1950s, the loss of this habitat, which had been maintained by rabbits, was bad news for the sun-loving red ant, *Myrmica sabuleti* and, in turn, for the large blue butterfly whose caterpillar is reared by the ants. As a result, the large blue became extinct in Britain in 1979.

Rabbit *Oryctolagus cuniculus*

Rabbits were introduced into Britain from France by the Normans, as a source of meat and fur. They were first recorded in the wild in the 14th century but numbers only grew substantially after about 1750, due to changes in farming and the increasing control of predators by gamekeepers. Their fur varies in colour but it is usually grey with reddish streaks on the back, and paler underneath. Dense, soft fur retains heat poorly when it is wet, so rabbits try to stay dry. Rabbits have a large number of predators and listen for potential danger. They are active during the day and usually stay within 200 metres of their burrows. Rabbit numbers have fluctuated greatly in the past; in the early 20th century there were around 100 million in Great Britain, but in the 1950s, the viral disease myxomatosis killed over 99 per cent of the wild population.

Head-body length	30-40 cm
Tail length	About the same length as their head
Weight	1.2-2 kg
Lifespan	Only about 10 per cent of wild rabbits survive their first year and few live beyond two years old. Captive rabbits can reach 10 years.

Reproduction: Rabbits give birth to three to seven young (kittens) per litter and, if the weather is favourable, females can have litters every five to six weeks from February to August. The young are born blind, deaf and almost hairless; they can open their eyes after 10 days and are weaned at about 25 days. They can breed from the age of four months.

Diet: Grasses, cereal crops, root vegetables and young shoots of meadow plants. In winter, they eat the bark of small trees.

Habitat: The most suitable habitats are areas of short vegetation close to woodland or banks suitable for burrows. Lighter soils and well-drained grassland support the greatest numbers of rabbits.

Predators: Foxes, mustelids such as stoats and weasels, badgers and buzzards.

Threats: Disease (Rabbit Haemorrhagic Disease and Myxoma virus).

Status & conservation: Non-native and common; no conservation listing.

Population size & distribution: UK population 38 million. The population has increased over the last 25 years but has fallen significantly over the last 10 years, especially in Scotland. Rabbits are widespread throughout Britain and Ireland below a height of 350 m, but are absent from the Isle of Rum and the Scilly Isles.

Did you know?

Two to eight adults occupy a warren with males and females establishing separate pecking-orders. Dominant males father the majority of offspring in the group, while dominant females obtain the best nest sites.

Brown hare *Lepus europaeus*

It is thought that brown hares originated in the grasslands of central Asia and were introduced into Britain during Roman times. Brown hares are much larger than rabbits and have tawny fur and very long, black-tipped ears. They live exclusively above ground, resting in shallow excavations, called *forms*, up to 10 cm deep. Speed is their main defence and they can run at up to 72 km per hour to escape predators. As they run, they tuck their tail down so that the white underside is not visible – unlike rabbits, which hold their tail up, flashing its white markings. Hares are mostly active at night and generally forage at dusk and dawn. Although they are mainly solitary, hares come together in small groups in late winter and during courtship, which often involves several males chasing a female.

Head-body length	48-70 cm
Ear length	About same length as head
Weight	2-5 kg (females are on average slightly heavier than males)
Lifespan	Typically two to three years; five per cent of individuals live more than five years. The oldest known wild animal was 12.5 years old.

Reproduction: Hares breed from February to September and females can have up to four litters per year, each of four young (called leverets) on average. Females look after the leverets on their own and the young are weaned after three to four weeks.

Diet: Grasses; young cereal and other arable crops. Shrubs are browsed in winter if snow makes grazing difficult.

Habitat: Mainly arable farmland; also grassland with sheltered areas in long grass, hedgerows and pasture.

Predators: Mostly foxes.

Threats: Agricultural intensification and hunting (both as game and as a pest when numerous).

Status & conservation: Non-native and common. Brown hares are a priority species in the UK Biodiversity Action Plan, which aims to expand existing populations. However, hares have minimal legal protection because they are considered a game species and can be shot throughout the year, including through their breeding season. They are the only game species in the UK without a closed season, when hunting is prohibited.

Population size & distribution: UK population 817,500. There is no clear population trend either over the last 25 or 10 years. They are widely distributed throughout Britain but almost entirely absent from Ireland and north-west Scotland. Hares are most abundant in lowland cereal-growing counties, particularly East Anglia.

Did you know?

During the breeding season, females fend off the attentions of amorous males by standing upright and striking out with their front paws. This boxing is the origin of the phrase 'mad as a March hare'.

31

Mountain hare/Irish hare *Lepus timidus*

In prehistoric times, mountain hares were probably found across much of Britain but today they are widespread only in Ireland and parts of Scotland. Irish hares are an endemic subspecies of mountain hares, native to Ireland, and more closely related to European continental populations than to those in Scotland. In the 19th century, Scottish mountain hares were introduced into England and the Isle of Man for hunting.

Mountain hares are smaller than brown hares and have shorter ears. They moult their grey coat in early winter, turning white to blend in with the snow on the uplands. They are very timid and mainly nocturnal, although they can be active during the day. If alarmed, they crouch motionless with their ears down and at the last minute, can dart away at high speed. They are mainly solitary animals but often graze in groups, feeding along well-trampled trails through long vegetation.

Head-body length	45-60 cm
Tail length	About same length as head
Weight	Weight 2.5-4 kg (females are on average slightly heavier than males)
Lifespan	Up to 10 years. Only 20 per cent may survive their first year.

Reproduction: Females typically have three litters per year between March and August. One to four young (leverets) are born in each litter, fully furred and with their eyes open. The mother suckles them for about four weeks until they become independent.

Diet: Mainly heather; also moorland grasses and other plants.

Habitat: Heather moorland, grassland and rocky hilltops, usually above 300 metres.

Predators: Mainly foxes; also wildcats, dogs, stoats and golden eagle.

Threats: Hunting.

Status & conservation: Native, locally common; vulnerable in England.

Population size & distribution: UK population 360,000 (Scotland, 350,000); Irish hare: Northern Ireland, 82,000. The population outside Ireland may be declining, but populations show large annual fluctuations. The number in the Peak District could be as high as 10,000 and is increasing. Mountain hares are present in the Highlands, Borders and south-west of Scotland; the Peak District and Isle of Man; and throughout Ireland.

Did you know?

Mountain hares have heavily furred hindfeet, particularly in winter, which act like snow-shoes, helping to spread the animal's weight so that they don't sink into soft, deep snow. Their tracks are characteristically broader than those of brown hares.

Carnivores

Members of the order Carnivora are predators and their teeth are adapted to a diet of meat. They have characteristically large canines for killing prey and *carnassial* teeth, one upper and one lower on each side of the jaw, that are specialised for cutting and shearing.

Carnivores are usually nocturnal and most have a characteristic style of hunting, such as pouncing and snapping in the case of foxes, or fast pursuit in confined spaces in the case of weasels and stoats. In Britain, they are often at the top of the food chain as they have few predators themselves, but many have been persecuted by humans.

Nine species of carnivore occur in the UK and another three, brown bears, grey wolves and lynx, are now extinct. Eight of the nine are native but one, American mink, is a more recent arrival, introduced in the last century. The nine species that are present today belong to three families:

the **canids** (dog family), to which foxes belong

the **mustelids** (weasel family), to which badgers, weasels, stoats, mink, otters, polecats and pine martens belong, and

the **felids** (cat family), to which wildcats belong.

Carnivores have a good sense of smell and use odours as a means of communication. Mustelids mark their territory with a musky scent from glands at the base of their tail. Polecats produce a particularly pungent odour, whereas otters produce a much more pleasant smell which has been described as similar to newly mown hay.

In the UK the law protects some carnivores that are exploited or persecuted, either for their fur or for hunting, or because they are perceived as dangerous. Wildcats, otters and pine martens are fully protected by law under the Wildlife and Countryside Act 1981, and polecats and badgers are partially protected. It is illegal to trap or kill these mammals without a licence. Badgers are also protected under their own legislation, the Protection of Badgers Act 1992, which also protects their homes (setts).

Red fox *Vulpes vulpes*

The distinctive red-brown fur and long bushy tail of the fox are a familiar sight almost everywhere in the British Isles. Foxes are intelligent, opportunistic and use a wide range of habitats, including towns and cities. They are social, living in family groups of a breeding pair, with cubs in the spring, and sometimes juveniles born the previous year that help with the rearing of cubs. Foxes dig dens (called earths) in banks or use vacant or occupied badger setts, or old rabbit burrows. In urban areas, their dens are often found under buildings or sheds, and in overgrown gardens and cemeteries.

Foxes hunt and scavenge with keen senses of smell and hearing, and probably use the latter to locate earthworms, which can make up a large part of their diet.

Head-body length	56-75 cm
Tail length	Slightly more than half the head-body length
Weight	4.0-9.5 kg
Lifespan	Maximum age in the wild is 10-11 years. In areas of population control, fewer than one per cent survive more than six years.

Reproduction: Foxes mate between December and February, and litters of four or five blind and deaf cubs are born between March and May. The young are weaned at four weeks and are independent by the autumn, typically moving away between October and January.

Diet: Almost anything from rabbits, field voles, earthworms and insects, to fruit and vegetables. In urban areas, they scavenge food from rubbish bins and gardens. Food is often stored to be eaten later.

Habitat: Most abundant in habitats offering a variety of shelter and food, including woodland, farmland, scrub and upland areas, as well as residential suburbs and gardens.

Predators: Few natural predators but cubs may be killed by badgers, dogs, and golden eagles. Most deaths are caused by humans.

Threats: Road traffic, accidental and deliberate poisoning, and shooting.

Status & conservation: Native, common and widespread. Hunting with dogs is illegal in England and Wales under the Hunting Act 2004 and is also illegal in Scotland.

Population size & distribution: GB population 225,000 (rural); 33,000 (urban). There has been little change in the population over the last 10 years. Foxes are widely distributed in Britain and Ireland but are absent from all the Scottish islands, except Skye and Harris, and from the Scilly and Channel Isles.

Did you know?
Foxes communicate with each other using a wide range of calls, facial expressions and body postures, as well as scent markings. The loud contact calls made by both sexes, particularly in the winter, include a blood-chilling 'scream' that may have inspired Irish tales of banshees.

Pine marten *Martes martes*

By 1800, due to loss of woodland cover, pine martens were rare in many lowland areas of Great Britain and Ireland; hunting and trapping by gamekeepers reduced numbers further through the 19th and early 20th centuries, and today they are still very rare. Pine martens are agile, cat-sized mammals, with dense, lustrous, chocolate-brown fur and a distinctive creamy-yellow patch on their chest and throat. They are solitary and secretive, and are mostly nocturnal, although in summer are often active around dawn and dusk. They are skilful climbers and spend much of their time in trees, moving quickly between branches, but hunt on the ground. During the day, pine martens rest on branches or in hollow trees, birds' nests, or in burrows amongst rocks. They are also strong swimmers. They have large territories that they mark with their droppings, which are often positioned in prominent places, such as the top of rocks, as a sign to other pine martens.

Head-body length	36-55 cm
Tail length	20-25 cm
Weight	1.3-1.9 kg
Lifespan	Up to 12 years

Reproduction: Mating occurs in late summer and females usually give birth to two kits or cubs in April or May the following year. The young are born naked and blind, their eyes opening at five to six weeks. They leave the den at about three months. Pine martens do not successfully breed until between two and three years old, which means that populations are slow to increase.

Diet: Mainly voles and mice, but also rabbits, small birds, birds' eggs, berries and insects.

Habitat: Woodland or more open ground with pockets of tree or scrub cover. In Scotland, natal dens are often in the roof spaces of buildings.

Predators: Fox and golden eagle may be the main predators.

Threats: Habitat fragmentation.

Status & conservation: Native, locally common in parts of Scotland but very rare in England and Wales. They are a priority species in the UK Biodiversity Action Plan and have been fully protected since 1988 under Schedule 5 of the Wildlife and Countryside Act 1981.

Population size & distribution: Scotland, 3,500; fewer than 100 in either England or Wales. In Scotland, their distribution is mostly confined to the northwest, and the population is expanding into Grampian, Tayside, Central and Strathclyde regions. In England and Wales, records are concentrated to the northwest of the Humber-Severn axis and the population seems to be being maintained by breeding rather than new releases or escapes of captive individuals.

Did you know?

Pine martens can leap up to four metres between tree branches and are adept at landing on their feet, unhurt, from heights of around 20 metres.

Stoat *Mustela erminea*

Stoats have short legs and a long, narrow body with a coat of sandy-brown fur and a yellowish-white underside. They have a bushy black-tipped tail, which easily distinguishes them from the smaller weasel. In Scotland, Wales and the west of Britain, the stoat's fur turns snow-white in winter and only the tip of the tail remains black. This white fur is known as ermine, hence their Latin name *erminea*. This fur was once used to make the ceremonial robes of kings and queens. Stoats are mainly nocturnal and are well adapted for following small mammals into their burrows. They bound along at high speed and stop every so often to sit up and sniff the air. Stoats are very playful creatures with an insatiable curiosity; they tirelessly explore holes, buildings and even people, if they feel safe.

Head-body length	16-31 cm
Tail length	9-14 cm
Weight	90-445 g
Lifespan	Up to 10 years

Reproduction: They mate during the summer and the following spring the females have one large litter of 9-13 kits, depending on how much food is available. Male stoats come into the nest when the kits are still young and mate with all the young females so that they are pregnant before they even leave the nest. Young stoats develop rapidly and are able to hunt for themselves at about 11 weeks old.

Diet: Mainly rabbits and small rodents, but also shrews, squirrels, birds and fish; occasionally birds' eggs, berries and insects.

Habitat: They are not fussy and will live in most places where there is sufficient cover and food, including woodland, cultivated land, hilly areas and grassland.

Predators: Foxes, owls, kestrels and occasionally cats.

Threats: Stoats are legally trapped and shot by gamekeepers because of predation of game birds.

Status & conservation: Native, common and widespread.

Population size & distribution: GB population 462,000. The population has continually increased over the last 25 years. Stoats are widely distributed throughout Britain and Ireland.

Did you know?

Stoats kill their prey with a swift bite to the back of the neck and have a fearsome reputation as bold, efficient predators, taking prey much larger than themselves.

Weasel *Mustela nivalis*

Weasels are Britain's smallest carnivore. They have small, sleek bodies with chestnut-brown fur, a yellowish-white underside and a short tail. They look similar to stoats but are smaller and lack the black tip to their tail. Weasels are solitary, elusive creatures, mostly active at night, and often hunt along hedgerows or stonewalls, sniffing out every hollow or crack. They are very agile climbers and also excellent swimmers. Whilst hunting, they often stand up on their hind legs to scan and smell their surroundings before dashing underground through burrows and tunnels in pursuit of their prey. Weasels must eat a third of their body weight every day just to stay alive. They become sexually mature at between three and four months of age and can breed in their first year. As a result, populations are quick to recover after periods when numbers have fallen because prey has been scarce.

Head-body length	17-25 cm (males are larger than females)
Tail length	3-12 cm
Weight	48-107 g
Lifespan	Up to three years

Reproduction: Mating occurs from April to July and females produce one or two litters of four or five kits each year, depending on the availability of prey. They make their nests in the burrows of other small animals, and the young are born naked, blind and deaf in April or May. In years when the vole population peaks, a second litter may be born in July or August, and those born earlier in the year may themselves have litters. The young are weaned after three to four weeks. Hunting behaviour is developed by eight weeks and the offspring disperse around 9-12 weeks.

Diet: Mainly mice and voles, but also rabbits, small birds and eggs in spring.

Habitat: Almost anywhere that provides enough cover and prey, including sand dunes, farmland, grassland and woodland.

Predators: Foxes, owls, kestrels and cats.

Threats: They are also killed by gamekeepers, although traps are most often set for stoats, which are more of a threat to game birds.

Status & conservation: Native, common and widespread.

Population size & distribution: UK population 450,000. The population has continually increased over the last 25 years. Weasels are widely distributed across Britain but absent from Ireland and some offshore islands, including the Isle of Man and the Channel Islands.

Did you know?

The weasel's head is the widest part of its body and if it can squeeze its head into a hole, then the rest of it won't get stuck.

Polecat *Mustela putorius*

Polecats have been recovering for almost a century, after heavy persecution by gamekeepers. Polecats have long bodies and short legs, with creamy-yellow fur beneath long, blackish guard hairs, giving an overall 'black and tan' appearance. They have characteristic white markings on the end of their snout and the tips of their ears. Polecats are mostly active at night and live in a wide range of habitats. They hunt mainly on the ground, relying on hearing and smell, and are poor climbers. Dens are usually in rabbit warrens or badger setts, or spaces under tree roots. When polecats are frightened or injured, they emit a foul smell from anal glands in an attempt to deter predators. This gives them their Latin name, *Mustela putorius*, which means 'foul smelling musk-bearer'.

Head-body length	30-45 cm
Tail length	12-14 cm
Weight	700-1,400 g
Lifespan	Up to five years

Reproduction: Mating occurs from March to April and a litter of 5-10 kits are born from May to July. Week-old kits have a thin covering of silky, white fur that is replaced with a brown-greyish coat at three to four weeks. Weaning begins at three weeks and the young are independent by two to three months old.

Diet: Rodents, rabbits, frogs and toads, and small mammals. Birds' eggs, fish, invertebrates and carrion are also sometimes eaten.

Habitat: Various habitats including woodland, coastal dunes, river valleys and often around farmland.

Predators: Sometimes killed by dogs and possibly by foxes and birds of prey.

Threats: Road traffic accidents; hybridization with domestic ferrets; poisoning from rodenticides; and trapping.

Status & conservation: Native and locally common.

Population size & distribution: UK population 38,500 (fewer than 500 in Scotland). Their distribution increased across England between 1992 and 2007, and since 1997 the population has increased by 22 per cent (mostly in England). Polecats are now widely re-established in Wales and central England. They are absent from Ireland.

Did you know?

Polecats seize their prey with their canines, killing it with a bite to the neck, which is perfected with practice. They can kill prey as large as a goose or hare.

European badger *Meles meles*

Badgers are instantly recognisable: two black stripes run the length of their white face, possibly a signal to warn off predators. They have short, powerful legs and strong claws, making them exceptional diggers. They excavate extensive burrows, called setts, made up of tunnels and chambers, sometimes at several levels, that are shared by up to two dozen adults together with cubs. In Britain, badgers live in larger groups than those in continental Europe and display a greater range of social behaviours, centred around the setts in the group's home range.

Badgers are crepuscular and nocturnal, emerging around dusk to forage and to groom themselves and each other. They use smell to identify others and to mark out group ranges. They are much less active in winter, but do not properly hibernate and emerge to forage in mild weather.

Head-body length	65-80 cm (males are larger than females on average)
Tail length	12-17 cm
Weight	8-12 kg (occasionally up to 18 kg)
Lifespan	Up to 16 years, but typically seven to eight years

Reproduction: Although mating peaks in spring, 'delayed implantation' mostly delays birth until February. Usually only one female in a group will produce one to three cubs. They emerge above ground at about eight weeks.

Diet: Mainly earthworms but also large insects, cereals, fruit and occasionally small animals, such as hedgehogs and rodents. They will raid bees' nests for honey.

Habitat: Most commonly a mix of deciduous woodland, open pasture and fields but also urban gardens and embankments.

Predators: Few natural predators in the UK but cubs are sometimes killed by dogs, foxes and other badgers.

Threats: Road traffic accidents and illegal persecution. Disease (gut parasites) can be a major risk to cubs in their first year.

Status & conservation: Native, common and widespread. Badgers and their setts are fully protected in the UK under The Protection of Badgers Act 1992.

Population size & distribution: UK population 300,000; the population has increased over the last decade. Badgers are widely distributed throughout Britain and Ireland but are scarcer in Scotland. They are absent from most offshore islands except Anglesey, Arran, Canvey, Wight, Sheppey and Skye.

Did you know?
Setts can extend over hundreds of square metres and have many large entrances. The spoil heaps outside setts, in contrast to those at fox earths, contain grass and other plant material, used as bedding.

Otter *Lutra lutra*

Otters are restless, playful and secretive mammals that spend most of their time along riverbanks. They have stocky legs, a long, streamlined body, and a broad muzzle with prominent, sensitive whiskers. They are perfectly adapted to a semi-aquatic life. Their webbed feet and long, muscular tail enable them to swim comfortably at about one metre per second and they will dive to catch small fish or to avoid danger. Otters can see as well under water as they can above it, allowing them to hunt for fish. From a distance, they can be confused with mink, particularly as they are found in similar habitats, but otters are much larger and, when they swim, they do so with just their head showing above the water, while mink swim with their heads and backs exposed.

Head-body length	59-110 cm (males, 'dogs', are larger than females on average)
Tail length	35-45 cm
Weight	7-11 kg
Lifespan	Up to 10 years

Reproduction: Mating occurs at any time of the year and females give birth to two or three cubs, usually between May and August. Cubs are usually born in a holt in a bank, or between rocks or tree roots. Newborns are only about 12 cm long but grow quickly and can swim at three months. They leave the protection of their mothers at 10-12 months and can breed at two years old.

Diet: Mostly fish such as eels, but also water birds, such as moorhens and ducks, frogs and rabbits.

Habitat: A wide range of aquatic habitats including clean rivers, lakes and coastlines; less commonly, marshy areas.

Predators: Few natural predators.

Threats: Road traffic accidents; drowning in fish and lobster traps; and pollution such as oil and PCBs.

Status & conservation: Native and localised. They are a priority species in the UK Biodiversity Action Plan and are classified as Near Threatened on the IUCN Red List (2004). They are fully protected in the UK under Schedules 5 and 6 of the Wildlife and Countryside Act 1981 and they are protected under the EU Habitats Directive and the Convention on International Trade in Endangered Species (CITES). Seventy-three sites have been designated Special Areas of Conservation specifically for otters.

Population size & distribution: GB population 10,300 (Scotland, 7,950; England, 1,600; Wales, 750) following virtual extinction in the 1970s. The population has continually increased over the last 25 years and their range is expanding in England.

Did you know?
Otters mark their territory with their droppings, known as spraints, which they leave at conspicuous sites along the water's edge. The spraints have an unusual sweet, musky smell that has been compared to the smell of jasmine tea or new mown hay.

American mink *Neovison vison* (formerly *Mustela vison*)

Mink are not native to Britain but were brought here from North America in 1929 to be bred commercially for their fur. Since then, releases and escapees have successfully established themselves in the British countryside. Mink have shiny, chocolate-brown fur that looks almost black, especially when wet, and a slightly bushy tail. Mink are mostly nocturnal or crepuscular but may be active at any time. They make their nests in existing burrows by the waterside, often between tree roots or in old rabbit burrows, which they line with dry vegetation, fur and feathers. They are agile climbers and good swimmers, and have a very well developed sense of smell, which they use to locate their prey and to detect threats.

Head-body length	30-47cm (males are larger than females on average)
Tail length	About half the length of their body
Weight	0.5-1.5 kg
Lifespan	Up to six years in the wild

Reproduction: Mating occurs in March and April and a single litter of four to six kittens is born usually in May. Weaning starts at five to six weeks and the young learn hunting skills from their mother before leaving the nest at 13-14 weeks.

Diet: Rabbits, small mammals, fish and birds such as ducks and moorhens, as well as invertebrates.

Habitat: Aquatic habitats, such as streams and rivers, reed-beds and estuaries, where there is abundant waterside vegetation for cover.

Predators: Few natural predators but otters, badgers and golden eagles have been recorded as predators in other countries.

Threats: Trapping and shooting.

Status & conservation: Non-native, common and widespread.

Population size & distribution: GB population 110,000. The population has continually declined over the last 25 years and may do so further as the otter population recovers. Mink are widely distributed throughout mainland Great Britain and Ireland, and are present on a few islands, including Lewis, Harris and Arran.

Did you know?

Studies of mink in the wild have shown that they can dive 100 times in a day, typically to depths of about 30 cm and for durations of 10 seconds, but dives of up to three metres and 60 seconds duration have been recorded.

Wildcat *Felis silvestris*

The biggest threat to the survival of the Scottish wildcat is the domestic cat, whose family tree split from that of other wildcats at least 130,000 years ago. The threat comes from interbreeding, mixing the genes of the two populations, which erodes the separate genetic identity of the wildcat.

Wildcats look very similar to domestic tabby cats but are larger, have a stockier build and a thick bushy tail with distinct black bands and a blunt black tip. They are solitary and territorial, mostly crepuscular or nocturnal, and use several different hunting strategies. Larger prey, such as rabbits, are stalked from behind cover when possible, before they rush toward the prey and seize it. Their dens are situated among large rocks on hill ground or between tree roots, or they make use of old fox earths or badger setts.

Head-body length	48-68 cm
Tail length	26-33cm (about half the head-body length)
Weight	2.4-7.5 kg
Lifespan	Up to 12 years

Reproduction: A single litter of up to seven kittens is born usually in April or May but can be between March and August. The kittens are born blind but covered in fur; they begin to walk at 16-20 days, play at four to five weeks, and follow their mother on hunting outings at 10-12 weeks of age. From about five months old, juveniles begin to establish their own home ranges and are almost fully grown and sexually mature after 10 months.

Diet: Small rodents, rabbits and hares, as well as other small animals and sometimes carrion.

Habitat: The edges of mountains and moorlands, where there is rough grazing and often woodland and crops. They avoid high mountain areas, exposed coasts and fertile lowlands with intensive farming.

Predators: Golden eagles, foxes, stoats and pine martens may take kittens.

Threats: Hybridization with domestic cats, shooting and snaring (despite legal protection), and habitat loss.

Status & conservation: Native and critically endangered; extinct in England and Wales. Scottish wildcats are a priority species under the UK Biodiversity Action Plan (listed as such in 2007). They are protected under UK and European law and the Convention on International Trade in Endangered Species (CITES).

Population size & distribution: UK population perhaps as few as 400. Scottish wildcats are present in central and northern parts of Scotland, north of the industrial belt between Edinburgh and Glasgow, but are absent from the Scottish islands and elsewhere in the UK.

Did you know?

Wildcats had died out in Ireland probably by the Late Bronze Age or Iron Age. In England, they disappeared from the south of the country during the 16th century, due to hunting and habitat loss, and were lost from north England and Wales by 1880.

Seals

The traditional view (based on fossil evidence) has been that true seals evolved from a mustelid-like ancestor, while sea lions, fur seals and walruses had a bear-like ancestor, putting the pinnipeds in the order Carnivora. However, genetic studies suggest that the group has a single, common ancestor, separating them from other groups, and they are so similar in their adaptations to an aquatic lifestyle that many accounts put them in their own order, Pinnipedia, which means 'flap-footed'.

Pinnipeds are highly adapted to life in the water: their limbs are propulsive flippers and their bodies are streamlined and elongated. They return to land (or ice) to give birth, however, and it is there that pups are suckled.

Seals are able to close their nostrils and ear holes when they dive, but like other aquatic mammals they must surface every few minutes to breathe. They are agile swimmers, using their hind flippers and undulations of their body to propel themselves forward, and manoeuvring with their smaller fore flippers. On land they are less graceful, hauling themselves forward with their forelimbs or using the rear end of the body to push off the ground.

Like all mammals, seals are warm blooded. They have a thick layer of fat beneath their skin, called blubber, which helps to conserve heat. The thick layer of blubber can account for up to 60 per cent of their body weight (in comparison, a healthy human has 15-20 per cent body fat) and, as well as providing insulation, streamlines their bodies.

There are only two species of seal resident around the British Isles, common seals and grey seals, and they live in different types of coastal habitat. Common seals prefer sheltered waters, especially mud and sandbanks, while grey seals prefer exposed, rocky shores.

Grey seals were the first mammals to be protected by law in the UK, under the Grey Seals Protection Act 1914. They are protected during their breeding season, making it illegal to kill them around the British coast without a licence, and no licences have been issued since the late 1970s. Common seals gained the same protection under the Conservation of Seals Act 1970. Both species are protected in Northern Ireland under the Wildlife (Northern Ireland) Order 1985.

In addition to resident common and grey seals, there are rare sightings of other pinnipeds in British waters, including ringed *(Phoca hispida)*, harp *(Phoca groenlandica)*, bearded *(Erignathus barbatus)* and hooded *(Cystophora cristata)* seals and the walrus *(Odobenus rosmarus)*.

Map just shows the coastal part of their potential range

Common (or Harbour) seal *Phoca vitulina*

Common seals are less abundant in the UK than grey seals. They have a dog-like face with large brown eyes, white whiskers and a snub nose but it can be difficult to tell the two species apart, especially in the water. Their fur varies in colour but is usually speckled grey-brown and may appear silvery when dry. Pups are born with a dark, adult pelage, their white fur having moulted while still in the womb. Although they live in groups of up to 1,000, common seals keep a respectful distance from each other, avoiding confrontation. They are unable to drink seawater and get most of their water from prey.

Head-body length	120-160 cm
Weight	45-130 kg
Lifespan	The maximum age of males is about 20 years, and that of females about 30 years.

Reproduction: Mating occurs in July and single pups are born the following June and early July. They are weaned after about four weeks, when females will mate again. Pups are born on land exposed at low tide and are able to swim and dive hours after birth.

Diet: Fish, including cod, herring and mackerel, as well as squid, shellfish and crustaceans.

Habitat: Sheltered rocky shores and sandy estuaries.

Predators: UK seals have no natural predators but attacks by sharks and killer whales have been recorded in British waters.

Threats: Pollution, disease (Phocine Distemper Virus) and entanglement in discarded fishing gear. The reasons for the current decline are unknown.

Status & conservation: Native and locally common, but recent declines since 2000 (of up to 50 per cent) have been recorded in populations in Orkney, Shetland, the Moray Firth and Firth of Tay. They are classified as Least Concern on the IUCN Red List and are protected under the EC Habitats Directive. Sixteen Special Areas of Conservation have been designated specifically for seals.

Population size & distribution: UK population 40,000-46,000. Abundant in northern waters but rare elsewhere. They are found around Orkney, Shetland, and the Outer Hebrides; a few colonies exist along the east coast in sandy estuaries, from Scotland to the Wash, and on the north and south coasts of Ireland.

Did you know?

During dives of up to 10 minutes, seals slow their heart rate down from 120 beats per minute to 40 bpm as the blood flow to their muscles is reduced to conserve oxygen. On deep dives, of up to 30 minutes, their heart rate may fall to 3-4 bpm.

Map just shows the coastal part of their potential range

Grey seal *Halichoerus grypus*

Globally, grey seals are one of the rarest seal species and about 50 per cent of the world population live in British and Irish waters. They have a distinctive horse-like face with a long muzzle, large eyes and long whiskers. Their fur varies from light to dark speckled grey or even black. Seal pups however are born with creamy white fur and stay on land for two to three weeks until they moult. A thick layer of fat just beneath the skin insulates both pups and adults from the cold seawater. Males breed with several females: some will try to defend an area around a group of females, while others try to control access to beaches, gullies or pools of water. As a result, the number of females that a male mates with depends on the size of the breeding colony and physical features of the breeding site.

Head-body length	1.4-2.5 m (average 1.8 m for females and 2.1 m for males)
Weight	130-440 kg (average 155 kg for females and 233 kg for males)
Lifespan	Few females live more than 35 years and few males beyond 20 years.

Reproduction: Grey seals usually come ashore to breed from late September until December. They prefer barren, uninhabited islands and often go back to the same beach each year to breed. They give birth to a single pup of about 14 kg, which the mother sniffs to learn its scent. Pups are suckled five or six times a day for 16-18 days, more than doubling their weight by the time they are weaned and have moulted their white fur.

Diet: Mainly fish, especially sandeels; also cephalopods (such as squid) and occasionally birds.

Habitat: Grey seals feed around rocky coasts, sheltered coves, clear waters and sandy bays of offshore islands.

Predators: No natural predators in UK waters.

Threats: Pollution, especially chlorinated compounds such as PCBs, entanglement in discarded fishing nets, and disturbance by tourists.

Status & conservation: Locally common. Increases seen in the 20th century are now levelling off. They are legally protected in the UK and under the EC Habitats Directive. In 1999, the uninhabited island of Linga Holm in the Orkney Islands was purchased by the Scottish Wildlife Trust as a sanctuary for grey seals.

Population size & distribution: UK population 200,000. Grey seals are particularly abundant around the coasts of the Outer Hebrides and the Orkney Islands in Scotland. Small numbers are found off the coasts of Wales, Cornwall and Norfolk, and larger numbers off the Lincolnshire coast, Farne Islands, Isle of May and Shetland Islands.

Did you know?

Blind seals are typically found in good condition, suggesting that seals can forage with senses other than sight, such as their acute sense of smell and perhaps with their tactile whiskers, which may detect pressure waves.

Deer and wild boar

Even-toed ungulates (members of the order Artiodactyla) are large herbivorous mammals that walk on two-hoofed toes (the third and forth toe), leaving tracks of two distinctive 'slots'. Artiodactyls include cattle, sheep and goats, and in Britain, there are seven wild species: wild boar and red, fallow, roe, sika, muntjac and Chinese water deer. Wild boar, red and roe deer are native, although from the 15th century until recently there were no wild boar in the wild. Fallow, sika, muntjac and Chinese water deer were introduced into zoos and wildlife parks but have since established wild, breeding populations in the British countryside.

Apart from Chinese water deer, adult males (called stags or bucks) have antlers during the rutting season, used to gain the attention of females or to defend a harem from other males. The antlers are shed each year, usually in spring, and are grown again within three or four months. In contrast to horns, which are made of keratin and grow continuously, antlers are made of bone and while they are growing are nourished and protected by a layer of skin, called velvet, with a rich blood supply. When the antlers are fully grown, the velvet is shed and males will scrape their antlers against trees to remove it. Older males have larger and more elaborate antlers.

Deer (but not wild boar) are ruminants, with complex four-chambered stomachs that enable them to digest a diet of plant material. They 'chew the cud', passing food back up from the stomach to be chewed a second time before swallowing it again.

Deer in Britain, with the exception of muntjac, are protected by the Deer Act 1991 which bans the killing of deer during particular periods of the year. The dates of these 'closed' seasons vary between species and for males and females.

Deer and wild boar

Red deer   *Cervus elaphus*

Red deer are the largest wild terrestrial mammal in Britain. The males have spectacular antlers, which branch out and can span up to one metre wide. They shed them every spring. The size and complexity of the antlers increase as the stag gets older. They are used as weapons during the rut but also act as a status symbol. Red deer have reddish-brown fur in summer, which becomes grey-brown in winter. They normally live in small single-sex herds and get together in autumn when the rutting season begins. Stags are very noisy during the rut and their bellowing can be heard from half a kilometre away. Females are solitary when giving birth, but then gather into herds with their young and non-breeding males.

Shoulder height	110-120 cm
Weight	Up to 225 kg
Lifespan	Up to 25 years

Reproduction: The rut, or mating season, lasts for about a month in autumn. Usually a single calf is born in May or June, but the incidence of twins increases in habitats with plentiful resources. The calf is born with white spots on its fur, but these disappear within a few weeks.

Diet: Leaves, grasses, heather, rushes and tree bark, especially in the winter.

Habitat: Forests, particularly conifer plantations in Scotland, but also open hillsides and moorland especially in Scotland and the Pennines.

Predators: No natural predators in the UK.

Threats: They are culled in some areas, particularly as they can cause damage to commercial tree plantations. Calves are most likely to die from cold and wet winters.

Status & conservation: Native and common.

Population size & distribution: GB population 350,000 (England, 12,000; Wales, fewer than 500). The population has remained unchanged over the last 10 years. They are widely distributed in Scotland (mainly present on hill land) and are present on some of the Scottish islands. In England, the main populations are on Exmoor and the Quantock Hills in Devon and Somerset, the New Forest in Hampshire, Cumbria, the Peak District, Cannock Chase in Staffordshire and East Anglia. They are commonly kept in deer parks throughout the country. Small populations occur in Ireland.

Did you know?

Red deer stags in woodlands and grasslands in the south of England usually produce larger antlers with more points than those feeding on poorer vegetation in the uplands of northern Britain.

Roe deer *Capreolus capreolus*

Roe deer are native to Britain and are the most widespread deer in the country. They are relatively small, about the size of a goat, which gives them their Latin name meaning 'little goat'. They have sandy red-brown fur in summer and rather grey-brown fur in winter. Females have a whitish patch on their rump (called the caudal patch), similar in shape to an inverted heart, whereas males have a kidney-shaped patch. They have a very small tail that looks just like a tuft of fur and have distinctive black noses and white chins. The males have short antlers, rarely longer than 25 cm, with a maximum of three points each. When cleaning their newly grown antlers, roe deer can sometimes damage young trees by vigorously rubbing them along the trunk and branches. In common with most small deer species, roe deer tend to be solitary animals.

Shoulder height	63-69 cm
Weight	18-27 kg
Lifespan	Most die before 8-10 years; the maximum recorded age in the wild is 14 years for males and 18 for females.

Reproduction: Roe deer mate in late July and August, two or three months earlier than other deer in Britain. The females often give birth in May or June the following year, often to twins. The young have a distinct line of white spots along their back and can totter around about one hour after birth. They usually lie hidden in the undergrowth for the first week until they are strong enough to accompany their mothers.

Diet: Bramble, oak, ash, wild rose and grasses in summer. Heather, acorns, ivy, ferns and coniferous trees in winter.

Habitat: Mostly woodland with low vegetation and clearings.

Predators: Occasionally foxes, eagles and wildcats.

Threats: Roe deer are hunted for their meat. Where roe and muntjac compete, muntjac are more likely to succeed.

Status & conservation: Native and widespread.

Population size & distribution: GB population 500,000 (Scotland, 350,000; England, 150,000). After nearly becoming extinct in England during the 19th century, the population has continuously increased over the last 40 years. They are now present throughout much of England and have recently colonised parts of Wales, but are absent from Ireland, the Isle of Wight and most of the Scottish islands.

Did you know?

In winter, when males have shed their antlers, it can be difficult to tell male and female roe deer apart. The best way is by looking at markings on the rump. Females have a distinct small tuft of white fur at the bottom of the caudal patch, whereas males have none.

Deer and wild boar

Sika   *Cervus nippon*

Sika are native to islands of Japan and Taiwan and were first introduced into deer parks and private collections in the UK in 1860, from where they subsequently escaped or were released. The colour of their coat varies but it is generally chestnut brown and spotted in summer and dark grey in winter. They have a characteristic white patch of fur, outlined in black, beneath their short white tail. Stags have relatively simple antlers which generally have four points on each antler. The antlers are cast each year in April or May. Sika are mostly solitary and are most active at dusk. Where they are persecuted, they become very sensitive to human disturbance and only venture into more open areas at night. Sika can cause damage to commercial forests when they gouge deep, vertical grooves into mature tree trees with their antlers, which they do to mark their territory.

Shoulder height	80-120 cm
Weight	40-60 kg
Lifespan	Up to 15 years

Reproduction: Mating occurs from late August to October and a single fawn is born in May or June. The young become independent after 6-10 months.

Diet: Mainly grasses, sedges and heather, but also fungi and bark.

Habitat: Coniferous woodland and heath, but also deciduous woodland.

Predators: No natural predators in the UK.

Threats: Many young do not survive their first winter because of exposure and starvation. Many populations are closely managed in an attempt to control numbers.

Status & conservation: Non-native and locally common

Population size & distribution: GB population 11,500 (Scotland, 9,500; England, 2,500); Ireland, 20,000-25,000. The population has continually increased over the last 20 years. In England, there are populations along the south coast, in Hampshire and Dorset, and in the Lake District and Lancashire. No populations are thought to be established in Wales. Most of the populations in England and Scotland are in fact hybrids of sika and red deer; those in the New Forest in England, and around Peebles and Moray in Scotland however are thought to be still purebred.

Did you know?
Sika are very vocal animals and both sexes make a sharp whistling call; during the rut, that of males becomes a scream which can be heard up to one kilometre away. The word 'sika' is Japanese for 'deer.

Fallow deer *Dama dama*

Fallow deer were introduced for hunting by the Normans nearly a thousand years ago and are now widespread throughout the UK. The males have characteristic large, palmate antlers, which are shed between April and June. In summer, their fur is usually reddish-brown, with lighter spots, while in winter it is thicker and greyer, with less distinct spots. They have a relatively long tail with a dark stripe running along it. Fallow deer are social animals and can live in herds of up to 50, although more usually groups are of three or four, and typically made up of an adult female with her offspring from the previous two or three years. Larger groups are mainly made up of a single sex. Male and females come together in autumn to mate. During the rut, males scrape the ground with their antlers to mark their territory and establish their status, and will fight with persistent rivals. Fallow deer can be confused with sika, because they both have pale spots along their backs, but the antlers of sika are not palmate.

Shoulder height	85-110 cm
Weight	40-80 kg
Lifespan	Up to 16 years but males rarely live longer than 8-10 years in the wild.

Reproduction: Fallow deer mate in October and November; females give birth to a single fawn, weighing 4-5 kg, in June or July. For the first few days of its life the fawn will remain in a safe place while its mother goes off to feed. She returns several times a day to suckle the fawn. After a few weeks, the fawn joins the social group and follows the herd about.

Diet: Mainly grasses, rushes and leaves from trees. Also acorns, berries and beechmast in the autumn, and heather, holly and bark of felled conifers in winter.

Habitat: Deciduous woodlands; also marshes and meadows. This is the deer most frequently kept in parks.

Predators: No natural predators in the UK.

Threats: They are culled in some areas to control numbers.

Status & conservation: Non-native, widespread and locally common.

Population size & distribution: GB population 100,000 (Scotland, 4,000; Wales, 1,000). The population has remained unchanged over the last 10 years. They are present throughout much of England and parts of Wales and Ireland, and are locally common in Scotland.

Did you know?
During the rut, males make short, low-pitched groaning noises to challenge other males and to impress the females. When these calls are analysed, it's been found that each buck has a distinctive voice and an individual pattern of groans.

Reeves' (or Chinese) muntjac *Muntiacus reevesi*

Muntjac are the smallest deer in Britain, about the size of a labrador dog. They originated in southeast China and were brought to Woburn Park in Bedfordshire, by John Russell Reeves in 1838. During the 1920s, some individuals escaped and muntjac are now well established in the wild. They have a deep reddish-brown glossy coat in summer, which turns grey-brown in winter. When they are alarmed, they raise their distinctive long, dark tail to reveal the white patch underneath. Males and females can be distinguished by the dark markings on their face. Both sexes also have conspicuous dark pouches beneath their eyes, which are scent glands and used to communicate with each other. Males have short, straight, antlers, which point backwards and which are cast in May and June and subsequently re-grow by the autumn. Males also have large canine teeth, which extend beyond their upper lip and are used when fighting other males. They are usually solitary, secretive animals, mainly active at night.

Shoulder height	45-52 cm
Weight	12-15 kg
Lifespan	Up to 19 years

Reproduction: Mating occurs at any time of year and females give birth to a single spotted fawn after a gestation of seven months. Fawns seem to survive even when they are born in harsh winter weather.

Diet: Leaves, buds, honeysuckle, hogweed, berries, acorns, chestnuts, seeds, bark and grasses.

Habitat: Dense woodland with low areas of shrub; occasionally large gardens or small woodland copses.

Predators: Sometimes foxes and occasionally dogs

Threats: Road traffic accidents; hunting; and severe winters.

Status & conservation: Non-native and locally common.

Population size & distribution: GB population 52,000 (almost all in England; several hundred in Wales and fewer than 100 in Scotland). The population has increased continually over the last 25 years. In England, they have spread northward as far as Cheshire and Derbyshire. They are absent from Ireland.

Did you know?

Muntjac often communicate by making remarkably loud barking sounds for 20 minutes or more at a time and are consequently known as 'barking deer'.

Chinese water deer *Hydropotes inermis*

Chinese water deer are not native to Britain; they were brought to Whipsnade Zoo and Woburn Park in Bedfordshire in the early 1900s from northeast China. Escapees successfully populated the surrounding area. Wild populations are also well-established in the fen country of East Anglia. Chinese water deer are the only deer species in Britain not to have antlers. Instead, both sexes have large canine teeth. Those of adult males can grow up to six centimetres in length and are used to ward off other males that enter their territory. During the summer, they have light chestnut fur, which turns pale grey in winter. Chinese water deer are active both day and night and often spend much of their time grazing. They remain alert at all times and rely on their sensitive hearing, smell and sight to detect any danger. They are solitary and territorial, and generally only form groups in winter, during the rutting season.

Shoulder height	50-55 cm
Weight	11-15 kg
Lifespan	Up to 11 years

Reproduction: Mating occurs between November and December and a single litter of two to six young is born the following May or June. The young fawns are able to stand up after about an hour and spend most of the next few weeks hiding in vegetation. The young have a darker, chestnut coat with rows of white spots on their back. They are weaned by the time they are two months old.

Diet: Mainly grasses, sedges, rushes, and leaves, but also willow and bramble.

Habitat: Most commonly found near reed-beds, swamps, marshes, rivers and streams.

Predators: The adults have no natural predators in Britain but young animals are sometimes killed by foxes, and occasionally by stoats and crows.

Threats: Road traffic accidents; cold, wet winters; and hunting.

Status & conservation: Non-native, uncommon and local.

Population size & distribution: England, 1,500 (a further 600 are confined to parks). They are absent from the rest of Great Britain and Ireland. Populations are present in East Anglia, Cambridgeshire, Norfolk, Suffolk and Avon, and have probably increased in size in recent years. These populations may represent a tenth of the world population.

Did you know?
Water deer can smell humans up to 100 metres away and will move off even if they haven't seen the person. They sometimes run like hares, flinging their hind legs up very high behind them.

Deer and wild boar

Wild boar *Sus scrofa*

Wild boar survived in England until at least 1300, but had been hunted to extinction by the 15th century. They are still common throughout continental Europe, particularly where extensive forests exist. Adults have dark, bristly fur that is particularly thick in the winter, while the young have a lighter coat with characteristic horizontal, brown and cream stripes. Their snouts are long and tapered and the upper canine teeth of males develop into upward pointing tusks. Older boars tend to be solitary, but younger animals often live in small groups either of males or of females accompanied by offspring. Males and females only come together during the breeding season.

Wild boar forage with their sensitive snouts and can have substantial home ranges, often travelling over large distances. When food is plentiful though, they will remain in one place.

Shoulder height	100-170 cm
Tail length	16-30 cm
Weight	Up to 150 kg, though seasonal weight losses and gains can halve or double their weight
Lifespan	Up to 10 years

Reproduction: Mating occurs in winter, usually in December. Sows construct a nest in dense cover, where a single litter of up to 10 piglets is born in March or April. They begin following their mother around after a few days.

Diet: Wild boar are largely herbivorous, eating broadleaved grasses, tubers, bulbs, seeds and fruit, but also carrion, invertebrates and small mammals.

Habitat: Deciduous woodland, but they can be found in cultivated regions if there is cover close by.

Predators: Historically wolves, but no natural predators in the UK now.

Threats: Unregulated hunting.

Status & conservation: Once native, extinct for 500 years. Existing populations are introduced and localised (escaped or released from farms).

Population size & distribution: England and Wales, population probably in the low hundreds. The population trend is unknown. Unchecked, the population is likely to increase but hunting may be close to keeping their numbers stable. There are three breeding populations in Dorset, the Forest of Dean and on the Kent/East Sussex border.

Did you know?

The wild boar is the ancestor of the domestic pig, and the two readily breed, producing offspring with the typical appearance of wild boar. Hybridization between the two makes the genetic identity of wild boar populations in Britain uncertain.

Whales and dolphins

Cetaceans are a group of marine mammals made up of whales, dolphins and porpoises. Like all mammals, cetaceans breathe air: they have lungs rather than gills, and must hold their breath when they dive which, in the case of sperm whales, can be for over an hour.

They are adapted to a completely aquatic existence, feeding, sleeping, breeding and giving birth in the water. A pair of broad, flat (boneless) tail flukes pushes them through the water with powerful, up and down movements, in contrast to the tail of sharks and other fishes, which moves from side to side. They have streamlined, torpedo-shaped bodies and lack external hind limbs.

Whales dive with a lungful of air, but their main oxygen stores are in their muscles and large volume of blood. After diving, used air is expelled through their blowhole (modified nostrils on the top of the head) as a cloud of spray. The size and shape of this 'blow' is distinctive enough in some species to identify them.

At least 27 species of cetaceans have been sighted off the coast of the British Isles – six baleen whales (Mysticeti): minke whale, northern right whale, sei whale, blue whale, fin whale and humpback; and 21 toothed whales (Odontoceti): sperm whale, pygmy sperm whale, northern bottlenose, Sowerby's, Blainville's, True's beaked whale, Cuvier's beaked whale, beluga, narwhal, long-finned pilot whale, killer whale, false killer whale, melon-headed whale, Risso's dolphin, common dolphin, striped dolphin, Fraser's dolphin, Atlantic white-sided dolphin, white beaked dolphin, bottlenose dolphin and harbour porpoise.

About half are poorly known (such as some beaked whales), only occasionally sighted or reported from strandings. Close encounters with them do sometimes occur though, such as that with a female northern bottlenose whale, which swam up the River Thames through central London in 2006.

Five species – bottlenose dolphins, minke whales, harbour porpoises, white-beaked dolphins and Risso's dolphins – occur in inshore waters. Three of the most commonly seen are described here.

Thirty-six per cent of the 115 species and subspecies of cetaceans on the 2008 IUCN Red List are described as 'vulnerable', 'endangered' or 'critically endangered', meaning they face a high risk of extinction in the wild, and another third of species are too poorly known to assess their status. They face threats from human activity, either from whaling, bycatch, pollution or over-fishing, which reduces the availability of prey. Cetaceans are protected by national and international laws.

Map just shows the coastal part of their potential range

Bottlenose dolphin *Tursiops truncatus*

Bottlenose dolphins may be black, brown or dark grey on their backs, with lighter flanks. They have a tall, sickle-shaped dorsal fin and pointed flippers. Bottlenose dolphins are highly social, intelligent animals, and individuals often co-operate in activities such as hunting, baby-sitting and defence against predators. They are most often found in small groups (of up to 50 animals), and alliances and relationships between individuals are complex. They are capable of problem solving and tool-use, and are inquisitive and playful, frequently seen riding the bow waves of ships and large whales.

Length	3.2-3.6 m (males are slightly larger than females on average)
Weight	Up to 650 kg
Lifespan	40-45 years (males); up to 50 years (females)

Reproduction: Mating occurs throughout the year but in British waters most births are between May and November. A single calf is born after a gestation of about 12 months and is dependent on milk for 18 to 20 months. It may continue to suck for several years while swimming, hunting and social skills are developed.

Diet: Fish (including haddock, hake, trout, bass and sandeels), cephalopods and crustaceans.

Habitat: Inshore areas include estuaries and harbours, with brief forays into fresh water. They are also found in more offshore waters.

Predators: Killer whale and shark predation is less common in British waters than elsewhere.

Threats: Boat strikes and entanglement in fishing gear, pollution and depletion of fish stocks.

Status & conservation: Native. They are a priority species in the UK Biodiversity Action Plan and are legally protected in British, Irish and European waters. Habitats in the Moray Firth in Scotland and Cardigan Bay in Wales are designated as Special Areas of Conservation under the EU Habitats Directive.

Population size & distribution: Several hundred are resident in British waters. Resident populations in the Moray Firth and Cardigan Bay, and commonly spotted off the coast of southern Ireland and southwest England.

Did you know?

Females sometimes act as midwives, helping during births by supporting the mother in the water or by pushing the calf up to the surface to breathe. One individual was observed biting through the umbilical cord.

Map just shows the coastal part of their potential range

Harbour porpoise *Phocoena phocoena*

Harbour porpoises are the smallest and most common cetacean recorded in British and Irish waters. They have a dark grey back with a small, triangular dorsal fin, and are generally seen in small groups (of less than 10 individuals). Unlike many dolphin species, harbour porpoises rarely leap out of the water or bow-ride, although they sometimes approach slower boats. They keep a low profile in the water, but their small size and characteristic rolling swimming style make them easier to recognise.

Harbour porpoises have virtually disappeared from the Baltic and are almost extinct in the Mediterranean. Populations in the Black Sea, North Atlantic and North Pacific are considered by some to be separate subspecies.

Length	Usually about 1.5 m but can be up to 2 m
Weight	40-75 kg (females are slightly larger than males on average)
Lifespan	Few survive longer than 12 years but can reach 24 years.

Reproduction: Mating occurs from April to September, with a peak in July and August, and single calves are born from May to August the following year. Mothers may produce milk for up to 11 months, but calves will start to feed independently at two or three months of age.

Diet: Small schooling fish, including herring and whiting, and cuttlefish.

Habitat: Commonly found in coastal bays and estuaries, and around headlands, preferring water 20-100 m deep.

Predators: Sharks and killer whales.

Threats: Accidental capture in fishing nets (they are particularly vulnerable to bottom-set nets as they forage near the seabed), pollution, declining fish stocks and hunting.

Status & conservation: Native. Populations in the Black Sea and Baltic Sea are listed by the International Union for Conservation of Nature as Endangered and Critically Endangered respectively, and they are a priority species in the UK Biodiversity Action Plan.

Population size & distribution: Population 386,000 (continental shelf seas from southwest Norway to Atlantic Portugal). Mostly present off the western coast of Wales, in Cardigan Bay, in the Moray Firth of Scotland, and among the Western Isles.

Did you know?

Porpoises can be distinguished from dolphins by their shorter face, which lacks a beak. Their teeth are spade-shaped, compared with the cone-shaped teeth of dolphins.

Map just shows the coastal part of their potential range

Minke whale *Balaenoptera acutorostrata*

Minke whales are the most likely whales to be seen around Britain. They are the smallest member of the baleen whale family (Mysticeti). Baleen whales have two rows of flexible plates with frayed edges (made of a horn-like material) along their upper jaw that are used instead of teeth to sieve krill and plankton from the water. Minke whales have black, dark brown, or grey backs and a broad, pointed snout. A distinctive feature is the white diagonal band on their pectoral fins. Between 50 and 70 pleats run along their throat, which allow huge volumes of water to be taken in during feeding. The flukes are rarely seen above the surface.

Baleen whales are inquisitive and often approach boats. Although they do not often bow ride, they will swim beside a vessel for some distance and can reach speeds of 12 knots over short distances.

Length	6.8-8.5 m (females are slightly larger than males on average)
Weight	5-14 tonnes
Lifespan	40-50 years

Reproduction: Mating takes place from January to May and most calves are born around December. Females produce a single calf that is weaned at four to six months, the youngest known weaning age for baleen whales.

Diet: Krill and schooling fish, including sandeels, herring, sprat and capelin.

Habitat: Over the continental shelf, often very close to land. Minke whales will sometimes enter estuaries or bays.

Predators: Killer whales.

Threats: Bycatch, commercial whaling and pollution.

Status & conservation: Native and seasonally common. They are a priority species in the UK Biodiversity Action Plan and are legally protected in British, Irish and European waters.

Population size & distribution: UK population 10,500 (North Sea, English Channel and Celtic Sea). Population trend is unknown but there is an indication that the population increased during the 1980s and '90s. They are frequently seen in northern and western coastal waters of the UK and are common throughout the Sea of Hebrides.

Did you know?

In Scottish waters, minke whales are sometimes seen at the surface feeding beneath flocks of auks, Manx shearwaters and gulls in late summer. This gathering of feeding birds is known as a 'hurry'.

Bats

Bats are the only mammals that can truly fly (rather than simply glide as flying lemurs do). The same bones that make up our hands are elongated in bats and covered with a thin membrane of skin to form wings, giving them their name, Chiroptera, which means 'hand-wing'. There are 18 species resident in the UK (17 of which have breeding populations), about a third of the total number of wild mammal species in Britain, and all belong to the group Microchiroptera.

All British bats are nocturnal and feed solely on insects. In order to forage and avoid obstacles in the darkness of night, bats use a technique called echolocation. They emit a series of high-pitched shrieks (mostly too high for humans to hear) and listen for echoes as they bounce back from trees, buildings, prey or other objects around them. From the strength and direction of an echo, the bat can locate an object's position and take the appropriate action. Just as humans (and many other animals) picture the world with light waves, so bats do with sound waves.

Each species uses distinctive calls to echolocate, at different pitches (frequencies) that are measured in kilohertz (kHz). With the help of an electronic device called a 'bat detector', which converts the ultrasonic calls into sound that we can hear, it is possible to identify certain species as they fly past.

Toothed whales (pages 56 and 57) and the common shrew (page 8) also use echolocation.

Bats do not make nests. They gather together in groups at suitable sites, such as tree holes or in roof spaces, called roosts. They have separate winter and summer roosts. In winter, when insects are scarce, bats hibernate to conserve energy. In summer, females gather in maternity roosts to give birth, while males generally roost on their own.

All British bat species are considered to be vulnerable and are protected under the Wildlife and Countryside Act 1981 along with their roosts. This means that it is unlawful for bats to be deliberately caught or disturbed by anyone without an appropriate licence.

Greater horseshoe bat *Rhinolophus ferrumequinum*

Horseshoe bats have a distinctive horseshoe-shaped flap of skin on their nose, distinguishing them from other British bats. The noseleaf is used in echolocation to navigate and to locate prey. They are relatively large bats and hang freely upside down, wrapping their wings around themselves like a cloak. They emerge from their roosts about half an hour after sunset and generally fly close to the ground. When hunting, they hang on a perch and wait for insects to pass before flying out to catch them. In the last century, the number of horseshoe bats declined drastically across Europe (perhaps by over 90 per cent in Britain) and although rare here, the population is of international importance.

Wingspan	35-40 cm
Weight	17-34 g
Lifespan	Up to 30 years

Reproduction: Mating takes place in autumn and females begin to form maternity colonies from May, typically of 50-200 individuals, but they can number up to 600. Usually a single pup is born in mid-July, the mother giving birth hanging upside down and catching the pup in her wings. Young are weaned by seven weeks. Females are not sexually mature until their third year, so populations can be slow to grow.

Diet: Beetles, including chafers and dung beetles, moths, crane flies and caddis flies.

Winter roosts: Comparatively warm sites, including caves, disused mines and tunnels; they frequently move between sites, flying up to 30 km to a new roost.
Summer roosts: Mostly in buildings with uninterrupted access to a large, open roof space.

Habitat: Woodland edges, rides within woodland, and along hedgerows, as well as scrub and pasture, often close to water bodies.

Predators: Barn and tawny owls, sparrowhawks and domestic cats.

Threats: Starvation in late, cold springs; and pesticides, which reduce insect prey.

Ultrasound: They echolocate at a constant frequency of 82 kHz that sounds like a series of continuous warbles on a bat detector.

Status & conservation: Native and very rare. They are a priority species in the UK Biodiversity Action Plan and classified as Least Concern on the IUCN Red List. Ten maternity roosts and 27 winter roosts are designated as Sites of Special Scientific Interest (SSSIs) and 11 SSSIs have been designated Special Areas of Conservation.

Population size & distribution: GB population 1,600-5,000. The population may have increased since 1999 but the trend is uncertain. Their distribution is restricted to southwest England and south Wales. They are absent from Scotland and Ireland.

Did you know?
Horseshoe bats perform a skilled and perfectly timed somersault as they approach their chosen resting site. They flip sideways and grab a perch with their feet whilst breaking their momentum with outstretched wings.

Lesser horseshoe bat *Rhinolophus hipposideros*

Lesser horseshoe bats are one of the smallest British mammal species, weighing about a third as much as a greater horseshoe bat and about the size of a plum with their wings folded. They have grey-brown fur and, like greater horseshoe bats, have a noseleaf, which they use in echolocation. Their wingspan is half that of that of greater horseshoes. They hang freely by their feet and will twist their bodies round to look about them before flying off. Lesser horseshoe bats hunt close to the ground, rarely more than five metres high and often snatch their prey off stones and branches. They sometimes take larger prey to a perch to consume it.

Wingspan	19-25 cm
Weight	4-9.5 g
Lifespan	Up to 21 years

Reproduction: Mating occurs from September to November and females form maternity colonies in late spring. Usually a single pup is born in June or July and is weaned by six weeks.

Diet: Midges, small moths, caddis flies, lacewings, beetles, small wasps and spiders.

Winter roosts: Caves, tunnels, cellars and mines
Summer roosts: Mostly roof spaces of large rural houses or stable blocks where they form tightly huddled groups to keep warm, particularly during bad weather.

Habitat: Lesser horseshoe bats feed mainly along woodland edges, pastures and wetlands.

Predators: Domestic cats and sparrowhawks

Threats: Starvation; and insecticides.

Ultrasound: They echolocate at a constant frequency of 110 kHz, sounding similar to greater horseshoe bats on a bat detector.

Status & conservation: Native, rare and endangered. They are a priority species in the UK Biodiversity Action Plan and classified as Least Concern on the IUCN Red List.

Population size & distribution: UK population 15,000 (equally divided between England and Wales); Ireland, 12,000. The population has increased since 1999. Their distribution is restricted to Wales, western England and western Ireland.

Did you know?
Unlike other bat species, horseshoe bats are able to wiggle their ears, and those of lesser horseshoe bats are particularly mobile, helping them to locate the precise position of prey.

Whiskered, Brandt's and Alcathoe bats
Myotis mystacinus, Myotis brandtii and *Myotis alcathoe*

These three bats were identified as separate species only recently, so similar are their appearance and behaviour. Brandt's bats were recognised as distinct from whiskered bats in 1970, and Alcathoe bats (described for the first time in 2001) were recognised as resident in Britain in 2010. They are smallish bats and fast, skilful fliers, emerging within half an hour of sunset to feed on insects in the air up to 20 metres above the ground. Their shaggy fur is dark grey or brown, appearing golden on their backs. Brandt's bats are slightly larger than whiskered bats and are thought to be less common and widespread.

Wingspan	21-24 cm
Weight	4-8 g (whiskered); 4.5-9.5 g (Brandt's)
Lifespan	Up to 24 years (whiskered); 20 years (Brandt's)

Reproduction: Mating usually takes place in autumn but can occur later in the year. A single pup is typically born in June or early July and reared alongside other infants in a maternity roost. Pups can fly by the time they are three weeks old and are independent of their mothers by six weeks.

Diet: Moths, other small insects, and spiders. Whiskered bats have more flexible foraging habits than Brandt's bats.

Summer roosts: Houses, barns and churches; they are sometimes found in trees and will use bat boxes.
Winter roosts: Caves, mines and tunnels. Whiskered bats prefer colder areas close to the entrance. Brandt's bats often lodge themselves in tight crevices.

Habitat: Hedgerows and woodland edges, often near water, gardens and villages. Brandt's bat is more often in woodland than the whiskered bat.

Predators: Domestic cats and dogs; shrews or mice have been reported to feed on hibernating bats.

Threats: Habitat loss (suitable foraging areas and trees for roosting) and pesticide use.

Ultrasound: Whiskered and Brandt's bats echolocate between 32 and 89 kHz, sounding loudest at 45 kHz. On a bat detector, the calls sound like a series of clicks, but are quiet and can be difficult to detect. They can be confused with pipistrelles or Natterer's bats.

Status & conservation: Native and localised.

Population size & distribution: UK population 64,000 (whiskered bat); 30,000 (Brandt's bat); unknown for Alcathoe bat. Populations appear stable since 1999. They are widely distributed in England and Wales; whiskered bats are also found throughout Ireland and in southern Scotland. Brandt's bat has only recently been recorded in Ireland.

Did you know?
Whiskered and Brandt's bats can be told apart most reliably by differences in their teeth and in the shape of their penis. The shape of the tragus (a small lobe on the lower rim of the outer ear) and the length of their claws are thought to differ too.

Natterer's bat *Myotis nattereri*

Natterer's bats look very similar to Daubenton's and whiskered bats but have a pink, dog-like face. The tips of their ears curve slightly backwards and are pink at the base and darker at the tip. They have sandy-grey fur on their back and white fur on their underside, which can be clearly seen at dusk as they fly above. The old name of 'red armed bat' was given because their pinkish limbs are visible through their wings, which are broad and slightly pointed. Their tail membrane is lined with a fringe of short hairs and often held downwards to improve manoeuvrability. They are able to hunt in confined spaces, taking insects from foliage as well as flying prey, and often feed over rough water, making very narrow turns amongst dense overhanging vegetation.

Wingspan	24-30 cm
Weight	7-12 g
Lifespan	Up to 20 years

Reproduction: Natterer's mate throughout autumn and winter and females form maternity colonies from May to July. Usually a single pup is born in June or July, and is weaned by six weeks.

Diet: Crane flies, midges, dung flies, spiders and other small insects.

Summer roosts: Old stone buildings, churches, gaps in the wooden beams of buildings, and hollow trees
Winter roosts: Generally hibernate from December to spring, commonly in caves, cellars and mines.

Habitat: Deciduous woodland and open water sheltered by tree cover. They can often be seen along roads lined with high hedges.

Predators: Occasionally barn owls.

Threats: Loss of roosting sites.

Ultrasound: The echolocation calls of Natterer's bats are quiet and can be difficult to detect with a bat detector. They have short calls between 35 and 80 kHz, with a peak intensity at about 50 kHz.

Status & conservation: Native and fairly common.

Population size & distribution: UK population 148,000. The population has increased in surveys of hibernation sites since 1999 but there is no clear trend from counts of colonies. Natterer's bats are widely distributed throughout Britain and Ireland, except for the far north of Scotland.

Did you know?
Occasionally, Natterer's are found hibernating in unusual positions - sometimes resting on their heads or lying on their backs.

Bechstein's bat *Myotis bechsteinii*

Bechstein's bats were more abundant and widespread in prehistoric times, and their decline is probably due to the loss of ancient deciduous woodland since then. They have long, distinctive ears (although shorter than those of the long-eared bats) which curl back slightly at the tips, a bare pink face and pale to reddish-brown fur. They emerge after dark and follow roads and hedges to feeding sites close to their roosts. Their broad wings enable them to fly slowly, snatching insects from leaves and branches, or from the ground. Bechstein's bats are found throughout central Europe (where they were first described by a 19th century German naturalist) but are rare throughout their range and are one of Britain's rarest resident mammals.

Wingspan	25-30 cm
Weight	7-13 g
Lifespan	The maximum recorded age is 21 years.

Reproduction: Mating occurs between autumn and spring and groups of about 30 females form maternity colonies in late April/May. The young are born in June and early July and disperse by the end of August. The males are solitary.

Diet: Mostly moths, also mosquitoes, small flies and beetles.

Summer Roosts: Mostly natural holes in mature trees and sometimes bat boxes. Rarely found in houses **Winter Roosts:** They probably spend the winter mainly in trees but they are occasionally seen underground, especially limestone mines.

Habitat: Mainly woodland but also found in parkland, orchards and gardens.

Predators: Few natural predators.

Threats: Habitat loss and fragmentation. Their rarity

makes them vulnerable to the loss of individual roost sites and foraging areas.

Ultrasound: Bechstein's are very quiet bats and can be difficult to detect on a bat detector. They have short calls that peak at about 50 kHz.

Status & conservation: Native and very rare. They are classified as vulnerable on the IUCN Red List and are a priority species in the UK Biodiversity Action Plan. They are protected under the EU Habitats Directive, and in 2006, six sites were designated Special Areas of Conservation specifically for Bechstein's bat.

Population size & distribution: England population 1,500. In 2005, just six breeding populations were known. Only one maternity roost and fewer than 20 hibernation roosts are known. The population trend is unknown. They are found mainly in southern England, Dorset, Wiltshire and Hampshire.

Did you know?
Like long-eared bats, Bechstein's bats capture most of their prey by listening for noise made by insects.

Daubenton's bat *Myotis daubentonii*

Daubenton's used to be called water bats because they spend most of their time close to ponds, lakes or rivers. They have shiny, red-brown fur with a pale underside and a pinkish, round face with a pink, hairless patch around their eyes. They hunt by skimming over the water's surface with a shallow wing beat, either grabbing insects with their large, hairy feet or scooping them up with their tail membrane. Daubenton's bats can fly at up to 24 kmph and are often seen an hour after sunset, circling over water. They often fly in straight lines rather than the erratic flight paths of pipistrelles.

Wingspan	24-27cm
Weight	6-12 g
Lifespan	Up to 22 years

Reproduction: Mating occurs during autumn and winter and the females form maternity roosts in late spring. A single pup is born to each female in June or July and is weaned by six weeks.

Diet: Midges, caddis flies, pond skaters and mayflies.

Habitat: Lakes, slow-moving rivers and ponds in open countryside; less common in urban areas.

Summer roosts: Tree holes, tunnels, bridges, caves and sometimes stone buildings.

Winter roosts: Underground sites such as caves and mines; individuals lodge themselves in tight crevices or against the wall. Very few individuals are ever located at the same site.

Ultrasound: Echolocation calls range from 35 to 85 kHz, with a peak at 45-50 kHz. On a bat detector the calls sound like 5-10 second bursts of machine-gun fire.

Status & conservation: Native and common.

Population size & distribution: GB population 150,000. The population may be increasing but the trend is uncertain. Daubenton's bats are widely distributed in Great Britain and Ireland, though are scarce in the north west of Scotland.

Did you know?

Daubenton's bats benefited from the extensive network of canals that was built in Britain during the Industrial Revolution. The canals and the bridges that spanned them provided perfect feeding habitats next to ideal roost sites.

Serotine *Eptesicus serotinus*

Serotine bats are one of the largest bats in Britain. They have dark brown fur, which is paler on the underside and on their faces, and very dark ears. They make extensive use of buildings and are thought to roost in them almost all year round, making them vulnerable to disturbance during building work. Serotines can often be heard squeaking loudly just before they emerge at dusk. They generally feed in woodland habitats and their long, broad wings enable them to manoeuvre skilfully amongst the trees and to dive quickly to catch flying insects. They also feed around street lamps or snatch insects from leaves or the ground.

Wingspan	32-38 cm
Weight	15-35 g
Lifespan	Up to 20 years

Reproduction: Females begin to gather in May to form maternity colonies and usually a single pup is born in early July. The young usually make their first flight at about three weeks and can forage for themselves by six weeks. The colony usually disperses in early September.

Diet: Flies, moths, chafers and dung beetles.

Habitat: Pasture, open woodland edge, tall hedgerows and suburban areas.

Summer roosts: Mainly houses and older buildings that have ready access to roof spaces or wall cavities. They are rarely found in trees.

Winter roosts: It is likely that most serotine bats hibernate in buildings, in wall cavities or disused chimneys, for example.

Predators: Occasionally owls but no regular predators known.

Threats: Loss of foraging habitat and disturbance of roosts in buildings.

Ultrasound: Echolocation calls range between 15 and 65 kHz, with a peak at about 28 kHz. On a bat detector, the calls have a 'tock-tock-tock' sound, like irregular hand-clapping.

Status & conservation: Native and widespread in southern England.

Population size & distribution: GB population 15,000 (England, 14,500; Wales, 500). The population has probably changed little in the last 10 years but there are indications that their range is increasing. Most records are south of a line from the Wash to South Wales. They are absent from Scotland and Ireland.

Did you know?

Serotines are able to eat large insects while in flight, manipulating the insect in their jaws and chewing off the hard wing-cases, which are dropped to the ground.

Leisler's bat *Nyctalus leisleri*

Leisler's bats are similar to noctules (page 68) but are slightly smaller, with longer fur. They have dark, golden brown fur that is particularly thick around their upper back, so that it resembles a lion's mane. They are particularly noisy bats and can be heard just before they emerge at sunset, especially on hot, summer evenings. They fly high and fast, and dive to catch flying insects. They sometimes feed on insects attracted to streetlights in quiet areas. In summer, the colonies are very mobile and often move to new roosts. Leisler's bats are migratory: one individual is reported to have travelled over 200 km in Britain.

Wingspan	26-32 cm
Weight	12-20 g
Lifespan	Up to 10 years

Reproduction: Mating occurs from late summer through to autumn. Males call to females, either from a perch or while in flight, with a song that is audible to humans, and acquire a harem of several females. In summer, females then form large maternity roosts in tree holes and each gives birth to a single pup in mid-June. The young are weaned and become independent by six weeks.

Diet: Flies, moths, caddis flies and beetles.

Habitat: Pasture and woodland, as well as urban parks.

Summer roosts: Mainly old woodpecker holes or natural cavities in mature trees. They are also found roosting in (old and new) buildings and in bat boxes.
Winter roosts: They are rarely seen in winter but are thought to hibernate in tree holes and occasionally in crevices in caves and tunnels.

Predators: Probably long-eared owls and kestrels.

Ultrasound: Echolocation calls range from 15 to 45 kHz and peak at 25 kHz. On a bat detector, their calls make a distinct 'chip chop' sound.

Status & conservation: Native and widespread; they are scarce in Great Britain and common in Ireland.

Population size & distribution: UK population 28,000 (Northern Ireland 18,000; England, 9,500). The population trend is unknown. In England, they mainly occur in central and southern counties. Only a single record is known from Wales. Ireland is a stronghold of the world population and Leisler's are the third most common bat species (after pipistrelle and brown long-eared bats) here.

Did you know?
Leisler's bats have thick fur along their forearm, which partly covers their shoulders. They used to be called hairy-armed bats.

Noctule *Nyctalus noctula*

Noctules are the largest and highest-flying bats in Britain and they are usually the first to appear in the evening, sometimes before sunset. The adults have uniform, golden brown fur and short, dark brown ears, with a distinctive mushroom-shaped tragus. Their wings are narrow and pointed, and they have a characteristic powerful, direct flight, with repeated steep dives when chasing flying insects. They can sometimes be confused with swifts as they fly well above tree-top level. Individuals will make several foraging trips each night but may feed throughout the night on insects attracted to streetlights.

Wingspan	32-40 cm
Weight	18-40 g
Lifespan	Up to 12 years

Reproduction: In late summer, males establish a mating roost, usually in a tree hole, which they defend against other males. They attract females with a series of shrill calls and a strong odour, and will typically mate with four or five females. Females give birth to usually a single pup in small maternity roosts the following June or July. Mothers leave their young in crèches while they go off to feed. The young are weaned by six weeks.

Diet: Moths, beetles, flies, midges and winged ants.

Habitat: Generally woodland or pasture.

Summer roosts: Mainly old woodpecker holes or natural cavities in mature trees; sometimes found in buildings during the summer.

Winter roosts: Trees, cracks in rocks; sometimes in buildings.

Predators: Barn and tawny owls.

Threats: Loss of roost sites in hollow trunks and branches of old or dead trees through woodland management; and loss of foraging habitat such as permanent pasture and woodland edges/hedgerows.

Ultrasound: Noctules echolocate at low frequencies around 25 kHz, just within the upper limit of human hearing, and they can sometimes be heard, particularly by children, without using a bat detector.

Status & conservation: Native and generally uncommon. They are a priority species in the UK Biodiversity Action Plan.

Population size & distribution: GB population 50,000 (England, 45,000; Wales, 4,750; Scotland, 250). The population has remained unchanged over the last 10 years. Noctules are widely distributed through England and Wales, up to southern Scotland, but are absent from Ireland.

Did you know?

Noctules may feed at any time in winter if conditions are suitable but can survive successfully without feeding for nearly four months and can tolerate temperatures well below freezing.

Barbastelle *Barbastella barbastellus*

Barbastelles do not look like any other species: they have a distinctive, flattened face, with broad ears that meet at their base. Their face and ears are black and they have very dark, silky fur that has white tips, giving it a 'frosted' look. They emerge at dusk to feed on small insects, often over water. Their broad wings enable them to fly slowly and skilfully, and to pick up insects from leaves or in flight. On the continent, they are known to be highly migratory and have been recorded travelling more than 100 km.

Wingspan	24-29 cm
Weight	6-13 g
Lifespan	Up to 24 years

Reproduction: Mating occurs in early autumn at the end of the nursery roost period and the females form small maternity colonies the following spring. A single pup (or occasionally twins) is born in July or early August and is weaned by six weeks.

Diet: Small moths, flies and beetles.

Habitat: Deciduous woodland, wet meadows and water bodies such as wooded river valleys.

Summer roosts: Mostly in hollow trees, under bark, and in roof spaces of old buildings.
Winter roosts: Caves, tunnels, cellars and hollow tree trunks. They frequently move between winter roosts and may forage in mild weather.

Threats: Loss of deciduous woodland habitat; and pesticides.

Ultrasound: On a bat detector, echolocation calls of barbastelles sound like short, hard smacks in fast and then slow pulses, at about 32 kHz.

Status & conservation: Native, widespread but rare. They are a priority species in the UK Biodiversity Action Plan.

Population size & distribution: GB population 5,000 (England, 4,500; Wales, 500). The population trend is unknown. Their distribution is wide but thinly spread in southern and central England and Wales. They are absent from Scotland and Ireland.

Did you know?
Barbastelles use different echolocation calls when commuting between sites and when foraging. In light conditions, they will fly with no apparent echolocation.

Common and Soprano pipistrelles

Pipistrellus pipistrellus and *Pipistrellus pygmaeus*

Pipistrelles were only recognised (by differences in the frequency of their calls) as two separate species in 1999. They are nearly identical in appearance and behaviour, although soprano pipistrelles are slightly smaller. Differences in range, habitat use and diet have also recently been found. Pipistrelles are amongst the smallest mammals in Britain, weighing about the same as a twenty-pence coin. They usually have dark brown fur and a slightly paler underside, and emerge about 20 minutes after sunset, flying quickly just above head-height in pursuit of small, flying insects. In a single night, they can eat up to 3,000 prey and travel up to five kilometres.

Wingspan	19-26 cm
Weight	3-7 g
Lifespan	The maximum recorded age is 16 years.

Reproduction: Mating occurs in autumn and females gather to form maternity roosts the following spring. A single pup, or occasionally twins, is born between early June and mid-July.

Diet: Midges, small flies, mosquitoes, lacewings and small moths, are caught in the air.

Summer roosts: Most often modern houses, in tight spaces beneath tiles, under roofing felt or in cracks in the walls, but also trees and bat boxes.
Winter roosts: Generally in small crevices in buildings, trees or bat boxes, but are rarely found in caves.

Habitat: Open woodland, farmland and suburban gardens; they often feed over water and along woodland edges and hedgerows. Soprano pipistrelles prefer to forage in habitats associated with water, such as lakes and riparian woodland, and may be more specialist feeders than common pipistrelles.

Predators: Domestic cats, especially in urban areas.

Threats: Susceptible to insecticides and chemicals used to treat roof timbers.

Ultrasound: Echolocation calls from common pipistrelles tail off at around 45 kHz and those of sopranos at around 55 kHz, with little overlap between the two populations. The two species also differ in their social calls.

Status & conservation: Native and common. Soprano pipistrelles are a priority species in the UK Biodiversity Action Plan.

Population size & distribution: GB population 1,280,000 (common pipistrelle); 720,000 (soprano pipistrelle). Populations have declined by about 55 per cent since the 1960s but more recently (from 1998) common pipistrelles have increased and soprano pipistrelles have remained stable. Pipistrelles are widely distributed across the country but may be absent, or only rarely present, on some of the Scottish islands.

Did you know?

In some studies of captive soprano pipistrelles, pups have been suckled by females other than their mother, but it is not known whether such wet-nursing occurs in maternity roosts in the wild.

Nathusius' pipistrelle *Pipistrellus nathusii*

Like common and soprano pipistrelles, a Nathusius' pipistrelle could fit into a matchbox, with its wings folded. They are slightly larger than the other pipistrelles, with broader, longer wings. They have shaggy, reddish brown fur and are paler underneath, with a dark face and ears. Their flight is slightly faster – but less manoeuvrable – than that of common and soprano pipistrelles, and insect prey are caught in the air. Nathusius' pipistrelles are migratory and, in mainland Europe, individuals fly many hundreds of kilometres in late autumn and spring. A small breeding British population is resident all year, probably topped-up by winter migrants from the Continent.

Wingspan	22-25 cm
Weight	6-15 g
Lifespan	Up to 16 years

Reproduction: Mating occurs between early September and November. Maternity roosts of up to several hundred females form during April and May (typically in wall cavities), and one or two pups are born to each female in June or July. The young are able to fly after about four weeks and are weaned by six weeks.

Diet: Midges, mosquitoes, mayflies, lacewings and small moths.

Summer roosts: Tree hollows, spaces in buildings and cracks in walls.
Winter roosts: In Europe, crevices and rock fissures, cracks in walls, caves and tree holes.

Habitat: Deciduous and mixed woodland, occasionally farmland; nearly always near water, hunting over lakes and rivers.

Ultrasound: Similar to common and soprano pipistrelles but their peak frequency is lower, at about 39 kHz.

Status & conservation: Native and rare.

Population size & distribution: No population estimates exist for Great Britain. England, 1,600; Northern Ireland, 6,300-18,600 based on bat detector surveys. The population trend is unknown. It is likely that numbers in Great Britain increase in late winter and decrease at the start of spring due to migration. They are widely distributed throughout Britain, but rare.

Did you know?
Nathusius' pipistrelles were first recorded in Britain in 1940, as vagrants, but their status was upgraded to winter visiting migrants as records accumulated. In 1997, a breeding roost was found and four maternity roosts are now known in the UK.

Brown long-eared bat *Plecotus auritus*

Brown long-eared bats are easy to identify because of their unmistakable ears, which are almost as long as their body. In flight, their ears are held upright, but they curl back like ram's horns or are tucked under their wings when the bat is at rest. Brown long-eared bats have long grey-brown fur. They emerge from their roosts up to an hour after sunset and often follow linear features such as hedges, streams or fences to and from feeding sites. They fly comparatively slowly, either catching flying insects or picking them off leaves or tree bark. Their flight is very manoeuvrable and they can even hover. Larger prey is sometimes taken to a perch where they are consumed while the bat hangs upside down, leaving piles of insect remains, such as moth wings, on the ground below.

Wingspan	23-28 cm
Weight	6-12 g
Lifespan	Typically 4-5 years in the wild

Reproduction: Mating occurs between October and April but fertilisation and development of the embryo are delayed until the following spring. Groups of 10-30 females form maternity roosts in late spring and, unlike other species, will share them with males. A single young is born in late June to mid-July and is independent within six weeks.

Diet: Moths, beetles, flies, caddis flies, beetles and earwigs.

Winter roosts: Caves, tunnels, icehouses, cellars and trees. They prefer to hibernate in very cold temperatures, often just above freezing.
Summer roosts: Frequently roost in houses, often in large open roof spaces of older buildings, and in tree holes and bat boxes. They generally roost singly or in small groups.

Habitat: Typically woodland and lowland valleys.

Predators: Domestic cats, owls and kestrels.

Threats: Habitat loss (and the loss of roost sites); and insecticides, which reduce the abundance of prey.

Ultrasound: Brown long-eared bats produce very quiet calls between 25 and 50 kHz and are often called 'whispering bats'. The calls can only be heard with a bat detector if the bat is closer than 5 m away.

Status & conservation: Native and common.

Population size & distribution: UK population 245,000. Surveys of hibernation roosts indicate a stable population in recent years. They are widely distributed throughout Britain and Ireland but absent from mountainous regions of northern Scotland and some Scottish islands.

Did you know?
Brown long-eared bats are the second most common bat in Britain. The most common are pipistrelles.

Grey long-eared bat *Plecotus austriacus*

Grey long-eared bats are one of the rarest mammals in Britain. They look very similar to brown long-eared bats and, even close-up, it can be difficult to tell the two species apart. Generally, grey long-eared bats are larger and have a darker face and broader tragus (a lobe that extends up from the base of the ear) than brown long-eared bats. Their fur is more grey in colour, although this can be misleading because brown long-eared juveniles are grey until about a year old. Whilst sleeping or hibernating, both brown and grey long-eared bats tuck their ears beneath their wings and leave only their long tragus exposed. Both species of long-eared bats usually feed relatively close to their roosts. They fly slowly and their broad wings mean that they are highly manoeuvrable. Their ears are very prominent and give them an unmistakable profile, recognisable even as they fly by.

Wingspan	25-30 cm
Weight	7-14 g
Lifespan	Typically five years for males and nine years for females; up to 12 years

Reproduction: Females only start breeding at two or three years old. They mate in the autumn and females form maternity roosts in late spring. Usually a single pup is born in the second half of June.

Diet: Moths, lacewings, crane flies and beetles.

Summer roosts: Little is known about their preferred roosting sites in Britain. There are records of roosts in attics of old houses and in churches, similar to sites used by brown long-eared bats.

Winter roosts: Thought to roost in underground sites such as caves, tunnels, and cellars.

Habitat: Thought to be similar to that of brown long-eared bats. They forage in woodlands and open meadows.

Predators: In Europe, predated by barn owls; domestic cats may also kill them.

Threats: Severe winters; and timber treatment at roost sites.

Ultrasound: Grey long-eared bats produce similar echolocating calls to those of brown long-eared bats: quiet (low intensity) calls that range between 25 and 50 kHz; they are often called 'whispering bats'.

Status & conservation: Although native and very rare, they are not a priority species in the UK Biodiversity Action Plan.

Population size & distribution: England, 1,000-1,500. The population trend is unknown. Grey long-eared bats have probably always been rare in the UK. They are only found along a thin strip of southern England, from coastal areas of Dorset to West Sussex, and are present on the Isle of Wight and the Channel Islands. They are unknown in Wales, Scotland and Ireland.

Did you know?
The ears of brown and grey long-eared bats are particularly sensitive to low frequency sounds, such as the beating of moths' wings.

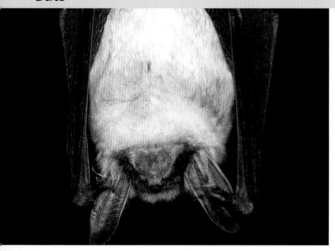

Greater mouse-eared bat *Myotis myotis*

Greater mouse-eared bats were discovered in the UK in 1958. Two hibernating colonies were found in the 1960s along the south coast of England, but the last record of a greater mouse-eared bat at the site was in 1988. In 1990, the species was officially declared extinct in the UK. In 2002, however, a juvenile male was discovered and has been recorded each year since. They are still present elsewhere in Europe, although their numbers there are thought to be declining.

Greater mouse-eared bats are the largest British bat species and the largest of the 11 Myotis species in Europe. They have broad wings and a body length of up to 8 cm. Their fur is a sandy colour and they have a bare pink face with large ears that have a prominent tragus. The paler fur on their underside can be seen when they fly, which often follows a straight path along woodland edges or hedgerows.

Wingspan	36-45 cm
Weight	28-40 g
Lifespan	Up to 18 years in the wild

Reproduction: Males mate with several females in autumn. The females form maternity colonies (often in attics) in March and each has a single pup from June onwards.

Diet: Larger insects, either caught in flight (such as moths and cockchafers) or taken from the ground (such as crickets and beetles), as well as spiders.

Summer roosts: Buildings and caves.
Winter roosts: Caves, mines and cellars.

Habitat: They are usually found around human settlements and hunt in woodland or over cultivated land.

Predators: Few natural predators.

Threats: Nursery roosts may be subject to disturbance or destruction (individuals are susceptible to the chemicals used to treat timber roofs).

Ultrasound: Greater mouse-eared bats echolocate using frequencies between 22 and 86 kHz, with most energy at 37 kHz.

Status & conservation: A solitary male is known from a single hibernation site, although the species is classified as extinct in the UK.

Did you know?

Greater mouse-eared bats have been known to travel over 300 km between winter and summer roosts.

Marsupials

Marsupials represent an early branch of the mammalian family tree – they have followed a separate evolutionary history to that of placental mammals for around 120 million years – but they are not, as was once thought, 'primitive' mammals. In many instances, evolution in the two lineages has converged on similar solutions to the problems of life in particular environments. The Australian dibbler fills the niche of small, secretive omnivores, which mice occupy among placental mammals; bandicoots have long, jumping hind legs and graze grass, in an equivalent ecological role to that of rabbits and hares; there is a marsupial mole and a marsupial anteater, and others that take the roles of burrowing herbivores (wombats), ungulates (kangaroos) and large carnivores (the thylacine and Tasmanian devil).

The word marsupial means 'pouched-one'. In many species, females have a protective pouch around their nipples, called a marsupium. The young are born at a very early stage of development, rather than continuing to develop inside their mother as placental mammals do, and crawl up their mother's body to begin to suck at a nipple. However, the mother produces milk for a much longer period than placental mammals do, up to nine months or more in wallabies.

Living marsupials occur in South and Central America, Indonesia, New Guinea and Australia; they make up over 300 species in seven orders. Only one, the red-necked wallaby, is found in the UK, a recent arrival that established itself in the wild about 70 years ago.

Red-necked wallaby *Macropus rufogriseus*

Red-necked wallabies are closely related to kangaroos and look similar, although are about half the size. British wallabies belong to a subspecies, *Macropus rufogriseus rufogriseus,* native to Tasmania, and escaped from private collections and zoos in the last century. They have greyish-brown fur and, as their name suggests, red patches on their shoulders. They stand on their powerful hind legs and support themselves with their strong black-tipped, silver-grey tail. Their ears, feet and muzzle also have black tips. Wallabies are usually solitary and active especially at dusk and during the night. They are not territorial and do not make dens, but during the day they will lie under cover in thick vegetation. They are generally secretive animals and are sensitive to disturbance.

Head-body length	60-70 cm
Tail length	62-78 cm
Weight	7-22 kg (males are much larger than females)
Lifespan	Up to 18 years

Reproduction: Females can breed from one year of age. A single young is generally born during the summer and emerges from the mother's pouch in May or June the following year.

Diet: Mostly heather, but also bracken, bilberries and grasses.

Habitat: Generally woodland and scrub, but feed out in the open, on heather moorland, for example.

Predators: No natural predators in the UK, but the young are sometimes killed by dogs or foxes.

Threats: Road traffic accidents. Harsh winters are also a cause of high mortality.

Status & conservation: Non-native and localised.

Population size & distribution: UK population fewer than 50 individuals. Three of the four free-living populations have become extinct in recent years or are no longer viable. Small groups are present in the Chilterns in England, near Loch Lomond in Scotland, and on the Isle of Man (along with Parma wallabies, *Macropus parma*); a large colony roams freely within Whipsnade Zoo.

Did you know?

When alarmed, wallabies (like rabbits) slap their feet on the ground for several bounds, warning others of potential danger.

Extinct mammals

Well over 99 per cent of the species that have ever lived are now extinct; but the pace of extinctions today is 100 to 1,000 times faster than that during most of life's history. It is as rapid as the extinction event that cut short the reign of the dinosaurs 65 million years ago. Around the world, between a quarter and a third of mammal species are at risk.

The history of the UK has its own story of extinctions and species such as the wildcat that have an uncertain future.

Britain became an island about 11,000 years ago and since then at least 11 mammal species have become extinct here. Environmental change was responsible for the loss of some: woolly mammoths, reindeer and root voles were seen off by a changing climate; aurochs (the ancestor of our domestic cattle) and elk died out as woodland was replaced with agricultural land. Others are only relatively recent departures: the brown bear and lynx survived to see the Romans; European beavers, grey wolves and wild boars became extinct in more recent centuries. For these species, hunting and persecution by humans, as well as habitat loss, were responsible for their demise. The case has been made for some of these to be returned to a wild state in Britain, reintroducing animals from surviving Continental populations, and a planned reintroduction of beavers began in 2009 at a site in Scotland.

Other species have started the business themselves: free-living wild boar in Dorset, the Forest of Dean and Kent/East Sussex are the descendents of escapees from farms over the last 30 years and, since 2002, a solitary greater mouse-eared bat, despite being officially declared extinct in 1990, has been resident in southern England.

Grey wolf *Canis lupus*

Grey wolves are the wild ancestor of the domestic dog and the largest wild member of the Canidae family, to which foxes also belong. They are similar in appearance to domestic Alsatians but have a broader head and a shallower chest. Wolves survived to the end of the 17th century in Ireland and Scotland but became extinct in England centuries earlier as a result of deliberate extermination by humans. They were once widespread across Europe but today, only a few isolated populations remain in forested mountainous areas, including ones in Sweden, Spain and Italy. They have nevertheless managed to spread back naturally to areas in Norway, France and Germany.

Wolves are social animals, living in groups of up to 14 or more related adults led by a dominant breeding pair, called the alpha male and female. Cubs born to the alpha pair are fed by the whole pack, which brings food back to the den. Wolves are mostly nocturnal and defend territories of several hundred square kilometres. Wolves hunt co-operatively in a pack, often pursuing prey over long distances until it is exhausted.

Head-body length	90-150 cm
Tail height	30-50 cm
Weight	20-80 kg (males); 16-55 kg (females)
Lifespan	Up to 15 years

Reproduction: Usually, only the alpha pair will breed. Mating occurs between January and April depending on latitude, and females give birth to a litter of typically four to six pups. Members of the pack share duties rearing the young, which are weaned at 8 - 10 weeks. Some juveniles leave the pack the following breeding season.

Diet: Mainly red deer, as well as roe, reindeer and wild boar; and smaller prey such as hares, birds and mice. They will also scavenge carrion. When native prey is scarce, they may turn to livestock, but in such circumstances guard dogs are an effective deterrent.

Habitat: Open woodland and tundra. They make use of natural crevices or gaps between tree roots as dens.

Predators: Few natural predators but territorial fights kill many, as do humans.

Threats: Persecution, as well as habitat loss and fragmentation.

Status & conservation: Extinct in the UK. Wolves are protected to some extent in most of Europe and fully in Norway, Sweden and Italy. Legal protection, land-use changes and shifts in human populations away from rural areas to cities in the last 40 years have allowed natural recolonisation of parts of Sweden and Eastern Europe from Russia and of France from Italy.

Did you know?

Wolves appear frequently in folklore, often as threatening characters but, while they do kill livestock, unprovoked attacks on humans are almost unknown.

Lynx *Lynx lynx*

Eurasian lynx are much larger than wild cats or domestic cats, with longer legs and a shorter, black-tipped tail. They have long, black ear tufts and a ruff of long hair around their neck and under their chin. In summer, their fur is a yellowish-brown, sometimes with distinct black spots and, in winter, varies from silver-grey to grey-brown. Lynx hunt by stealth on the ground or by pouncing from a low branch, and are dependent on woodland cover to ambush their prey, as well as for dens.

Lynx probably became extinct in Britain around 450-600 CE, hunted for their fur and to protect livestock. There is interest in the return of lynx to Britain and, among the large carnivores, it is considered the best candidate for reintroduction.

Head-body length	80-130 cm
Tail height	About a fifth of the head-body length
Weight	18-30 kg (males are slightly larger than females on average)
Lifespan	Up to 17 years in the wild

Reproduction: Lynx breed from January to April and females produce a litter of usually two or three kittens in summer, which stay with their mother through their first winter. Kittens are weaned after five or six months.

Diet: Mainly small deer such as roe (but also young red deer and reindeer) and chamois (mountain goats); also lagomorphs, rodents and ground birds less frequently.

Habitat: Coniferous forest; in Spain, it also lives in lowland scrub.

Predators: Few natural predators but birds of prey may take young animals.

Threats: Habitat loss and persecution.

Status & conservation: Extinct in Britain and Ireland. Once widespread across western Europe, lynx survive in Scandinavia, the Pyrenees and Balkans today. They are legally protected in most European countries and by the Convention on International Trade of Endangered Species (CITES). Reintroductions have been successful in Austria, France, Germany, Italy, Slovenia and Switzerland.

Did you know?

Lynx produce a variety of sounds but outside the breeding season, they rarely raise their voices. They have been observed to mew, hiss, growl, and purr, and (like domestic cats) will 'chatter' at prey that is just out of reach.

Brown bear *Ursus arctos*

Brown bears are thought to have become extinct in England in Roman times but may have survived later in Scotland. The last records from Ireland date from the Neolithic. The loss of deciduous woodland and an increase in agriculture are thought to have contributed to their extinction. Today, their distribution in Europe is similar to that of lynx and includes Scandinavia, the Balkans and European Russia.

Brown bears are large, mostly solitary and crepuscular or nocturnal omnivores. They have a prominent shoulder hump, a short (barely visible) tail and short rounded ears. During winter, brown bears hibernate in dens, either in a rock crevice or dug into a sheltered slope, but are easily roused during this period. Adult males are particularly aggressive, standing up on their hind legs to intimidate rivals.

Head-body length	1.5-2.8 m
Weight	135-545 kg (male); 80-250 kg (female)
Lifespan	Over 30 years

Reproduction: Cubs (usually twins) are born between January and March during hibernation, after a gestation of seven to eight months, and weighing only about 350 g. They are weaned at five months.

Diet: Mainly berries, roots, grasses and nuts but they will also scavenge carrion and kill prey up to the size of deer and bison. They can be skilled at catching fish.

Habitat: Mixed woodland, also open tundra and pasture.

Predators: Few natural predators.

Threats: Habitat loss and fragmentation, and hunting.

Status & conservation: Extinct in Britain and Ireland. They are a European Protected Species and have been reintroduced into Austria and Italy.

Did you know?

Brown bears will gain up to 180 kg of fat in preparation for winter. Females give birth and suckle their cubs during hibernation and may lose 40 per cent of their body weight during this period.

Elk *Alces alces*

Elk are generally thought to have become extinct in Britain during Mesolithic times but remains found in Scotland date from more recently (about 4,000 years ago), and it is possible that elk survived there into Roman times. Humans are the likely cause of their extinction, through hunting and changes in the habitat due to farming. Modern-day elk are present across northern and eastern Europe, including Scandinavia, Poland and northern Russia, and throughout Siberia. In North America, the species is known as the moose but there is debate as to whether in fact the two constitute separate species.

Elk are the largest living deer, with long legs and high shoulders. They have an over-hanging muzzle and a flap of skin, called the 'bell', that hangs beneath the throat. Males grow antlers during the summer for the rutting period in September – those of mature males are usually flattened and palmate and can be up to 2 m across. Elk are generally solitary and active mainly during the day. They feed along waterways and often wade deeply into rivers and lakes. As well as being strong swimmers, they can run at speeds of up to 56 km per hour.

Head-body length	240-310 cm
Shoulder height	140-235 cm
Weight	200-825 kg
Lifespan	15-25 years

Reproduction: Mating occurs in September and October, with males competing for females. Successful males mate with several females. A single calf or twins are born at the end of May or in early June.

Diet: Deciduous trees and waterside vegetation; in winter, they eat the shoots and bark of trees, and conifer foliage.

Habitat: Elk are most abundant where there is a mixture of forest and open ground, and prefer habitats close to water.

Predators: Wolves and brown bear, especially preying on females and calves.

Threats: Hunting – as game and as a pest; and traffic collisions.

Status & conservation: Extinct in the UK; elsewhere they are classified as Least Concern on the IUCN Red List.

Did you know?

In 2007, two elk, a male and female, were introduced onto the Alladale Estate and Wildlife Reserve in Scotland. The project's long-term goal is to restore the native habitat and reintroduce elk along with predators such as lynx and grey wolves.

Glossary

Adaptation The process by which organisms change by natural selection. It can also refer to a particular characteristic or feature that helps an animal to survive and reproduce in the environment in which it evolved.

Arboreal Living or active in trees, e.g. hazel dormice and pine martens.

Biodiversity The variety of species and communities in nature, and of genes and populations within species.

Buck The adult male of some species, especially rabbits, roe and fallow deer.

Carnivorous Describing an animal (or plant) that feeds mainly on other animals.

Colony A group of organisms of the same species living together or sharing a home.

Courtship The behaviour of animals to attract a mate (breeding partner).

Crepuscular Active mainly at dawn and dusk, during twilight.

Deciduous Trees that shed their leaves each autumn.

Dispersal The movement of organisms away from their parent or birthplace to set up home or become established elsewhere.

Diurnal Active mainly during daylight hours.

Drey The nest built by a red or grey squirrel, usually high in the branches of a tall tree.

Echolocation The means by which some bats and cetaceans navigate and find their prey, similar to 'sonar'. The echoes of high-pitched cries are used to identify obstacles in their surroundings.

Endemic Unique to a particular region, found nowhere else.

Feral Describes domesticated animals that are living in the wild.

Genus The taxonomic group above species. It forms the first part of the scientific name.

Habitat The environment in which an organism lives; woodland, arable, coastal and urban habitats are some of those in the UK.

Herbivorous Describing an animal that eats mainly plants.

Hibernation An inactive state adopted by some animals in winter when it is cold and food is scarce. Hibernating animals slow their heart rate and metabolism to conserve energy.

Holt The den of an otter.

Hybridization The mixing of genes from two distinct populations or species by interbreeding. Hybridization can be a problem in conservation (for example for Scottish wildcats, which can breed with domestic cats) because genetic identity and diversity are lost.

Insectivorous Describing an animal (or plant) that feeds mainly on insects.

Invertebrate An animal that does not have a backbone, such as insects, earthworms and crustaceans.

IUCN The International Union for Conservation of Nature.

Lodge The den of a beaver.

Mysticeti Baleen whales. One of two groups that make up the order Cetacea, along with Odontoceti.

Native For British mammals, a species is native if it was present when Britain became isolated from the continent, about 11,000 years ago, when the sea-level rose. Non-native species are those that have arrived since then, often introduced by humans, either accidentally or deliberately.

Odontoceti Toothed whales, including dolphins and porpoises.

Palmate When referring to antlers, having the shape of a hand with out-stretched fingers.

Pelage The hairy coat of a mammal, equivalent to a bird's plumage.

Riparian Living beside rivers or streams, e.g. otters and water voles.

Rut The mating season of deer; males compete with each other to obtain females with which to breed, often sparring with their antlers.

Scats The droppings of some animals, including foxes and pine martens.

Species A group of organisms that are able to breed with each other (producing offspring that themselves are able to breed); they represent a more or less contained 'gene pool'.

Spraint The dropping of an otter.

Subspecies An isolated population or regional variation of a species. Orkney voles (*Microtus arvalis orcadensis*) are a subspecies of common voles (*Microtus arvalis*), and Irish hares (*Lepus timidus hibernicus*) are a subspecies of mountain hares, for example.

Taxonomy The classification of organisms into groups that share characteristics and a common ancestry. Taxonomic groups (such as order, genus and species) are arranged in levels, each one containing the groups below it.

Territory An area actively defended by an animal against other individuals of the same species for food or other resources.

Tragus A soft cartilaginous lobe in front of the external opening of the ear. In bats it is thought to be involved in echolocation, but the precise way in which this works is unknown.

UKBAP UK Biodiversity Action Plan. This is the UK government's response to the 1992 Convention on Biological Diversity, which puts in place a framework for conservation efforts. In 2007, 1,150 species were listed as priorities for conservation, including 18 terrestrial and 21 marine mammals.

Ungulate A hoofed mammal such as deer and wild boars, which have an even number of toes (in the order Artiodactyla), and horses and rhinoceroses, which have an odd number of toes (in the order Perissodactyla).

Vertebrate An animal that has a backbone – mammals, birds, reptiles, amphibians and fish.

Scientific names

Different people call things by different names and, within the living world, it is no exception. Common names for species are numerous; they are often colloquialisms and folk-names, particular to dialects and regions, and it can be difficult sometimes to know exactly what is being talked about. It was the Swedish botanist Carl Linnaeus who, in his *Species Plantarum* and the tenth edition of *Systema Naturae*, published in the 1750s, laid out a system for naming living organisms. It is still used today and enables naturalists the world over to refer to a species unambiguously.

Take our own species name: *Homo sapiens*. The two-part moniker (italicised and Latinate) is the tip of a long tail of names, but it is sufficient on its own to identify us alone among the tens of millions of species. The hierarchy of names, ending with that of species (*sapiens*, without a capital) and rising through genus (*Homo*), family (Hominidae), order (Primates), class (Mammalia), and phylum (Chordata) to kingdom (Animalia), identifies groups that each encompass the one below and can share (with others of equal rank) the group above, marking their place in the grand scheme of things.

Still smaller divisions than that of species are sometimes recognised (distinct populations of species such as Orkney voles, a subspecies of common vole, or Irish hares, a subspecies of mountain hare) but 'species' form a natural unit of classification.

Linnaeus' taxonomy classifies organisms by their similarities, placing like-organisms together, and groups with similar groups. But similarities run in families, and in the light of Darwin's idea of descent from a common ancestor, classification does something more: it says something about the relationships between things. It can explain the patterns we see.

How many species are there? The number of species that are known stands at about two million; the number of living species in total, largely unrecorded and un-named, is thought by most biologists to be between five and 30 million. For those that are known, over 99 per cent are recognised only by a scientific name and a brief description of specimens in a museum. Another 250,000 species are known from fossils.

Worldwide, there are around 4,680 species of mammal, of which about 235 are present in Europe. One in six European species (15 per cent) faces extinction in the wild.

Further reading

Comprehensive and authoritative:
Mammals of the British Isles: Handbook, 4th edition, edited by S. Harris & D. W. Yalden. (The Mammal Society, 2008).

The New Encyclopedia of Mammals, edited by David Macdonald. (Oxford University Press, 2001).

Wider aspects of mammalian biology:
Collins European Mammals: Evolution and Behaviour by David Macdonald. (HarperCollins, 1995). Currently out of print.

Population estimates and trends:
UK Mammals: Species Status and Population Trends, edited and compiled by Jessamy Battersby. (JNCC/Tracking Mammals Partnership, 2005, available to download free at: www.jncc.gov.uk/pdf/pub05_ukmammals_speciesstatusText_final.pdf)

Single species accounts:
The *British Natural History Series,* published by Whittet Books, has several informative and readable accounts of individual mammal species or species groups, including *The New Hedgehog Book* by Pat Morris, *Dormice* by Pat Morris, *Badgers* by Michael Clark, *Bats* by Phil Richardson, *Urban Foxes* by Stephen Harris and Phil Baker and *Seals* by Sheila Anderson. The full list of titles is available at: www.whittetbooks.com.

More information about many mammal species is available at our website www.ptes.org.

Index

Acknowledgements

Picture credits: Front cover harvest mouse - Andrew Price; hedgehog - Stephen Oliver; pine marten - Laurie Campbell; back cover bottlenose dolphin - Laurie Campbell; hedgehog, mole, grey squirrel, European beaver, pine marten, European badger, wildcat, roe deer, sika deer, Reeves' muntjac, bottlenose dolphin, minke whale, brown bear - Laurie Campbell; common shrew, water shrew, lesser white-toothed shrew, bank vole, field vole, Orkney vole, edible dormouse, black rat, lesser horseshoe bat, Natterer's bat, Bechstein's bat, Daubenton's bat, Leisler's bat, common pipistrelle bat, Nathusius' pipistrelle - Pat Morris; water vole, mountain hare, stoat, American mink, fallow deer, grey wolf, Eurasian lynx - Terry Whittaker; pygmy shrew - Peter Oakenfull; wood mouse, yellow-necked mouse, house mouse, brown rat - Dave Bevan; harvest mouse - Andrew Price; hazel dormouse - Hattie Spray; rabbit, red fox, weasel, red deer - Stephen Oliver; brown hare - Robin Hamilton; polecat - Susan Sharafi; otter, common seal, grey seal, red squirrel - Niall Benvie; Chinese water deer - Geoff du Feu/Ardea; wild boar - Stefan Meyers/Ardea; harbour porpoise - M. Watson/Ardea; greater horseshoe bat - Gareth Jones/Bat Conservation Trust; whiskered bat, barbastelle, noctule, serotine, brown long-eared bat, grey long-eared bat - Hugh Clark/Bat Conservation Trust; greater mouse-eared bat - John Black/Bat Conservation Trust; red-necked wallaby - Steffen & Alexandra Sailer/Ardea; elk - Tom & Pat Leeson/Ardea; mountain hare in snow - Eric Dragesco/Ardea.

Track illustrations: Christine Oines.

Distribution maps: Based on material supplied by Midsummer Books Ltd and Bright Star Publishing Ltd from *Wildlife of Britain*, © Midsummer Books Ltd and Bright Star Publishing Ltd.

Grateful thanks are extended to: Pat Morris for his advice on an earlier edition of this book and for writing the preface; Sheila Anderson; Johnny Birks; Lisa Hundt at the Bat Conservation Trust; Jim Jones; David Mallon; Andy Purvis; Sandra Baker, Christina Buesching, Amy Dickman, Paul Johnson, Jorgelina Marino and Chris Newman at WildCRU, University of Oxford. Martin Noble, David Orme and Derek Yalden read drafts of sections or species accounts – their comments and suggestions greatly improved the text.

Many thanks to Zoe Roden, Hannah Stockwell, Jill Nelson and Christine Beadle for their help and advice with this revised edition.